A Plaza Wedding

A PLAZA WEDDING

Inspiration and Ideas

for the Wedding of Your Dreams

The pleasure of your company
is requested at the marriage of
Miss Alexandra Marie Garcia
to
Mr. Steven Allan Cushen
Saturday, the sixth of June
at seven o'clock
The Plaza
New York

FRED MARCUS

LAWRENCE D. HARVEY

EXECUTIVE DIRECTOR OF CATERING
THE PLAZA HOTEL, NEW YORK

A FAIRMONT MANAGED HOTEL
AMERICA'S GRAND HOTELS, SINCE 1907

VILLARD BOOKS NEW YORK

TEXT BY JANE KAGAN VITIELLO

DESIGN BY JOEL AVIROM AND JASON SNYDER
DESIGN ASSISTANT: MEGHAN DAY HEALEY

Library of Congress Cataloging-in-Publication Data
Harvey, Lawrence D.
A Plaza wedding/by Lawrence D. Harvey.
p.   cm.
ISBN 0-679-43772-X
1. Weddings.   I. Plaza Hotel (New York, N.Y.)   II. Title.
BJ2051.H37   1995
395'.22—dc20   95-13737

Printed and bound in Italy
24689753
First Edition

HOTELS • ATOP NOB HILL • SAN FRANCISCO, CALIFORNIA 94108

FAIRMONT HOTEL MANAGEMENT L.P.

ROBERT I. SMALL
PRESIDENT AND
CHIEF EXECUTIVE OFFICER

As President and Chief Executive Officer of The Fairmont Hotels, it is my honor and pleasure to welcome one of the most legendary hotels in the world, The Plaza in New York, to our family of America's Grand Hotels. The Plaza opened its luxurious doors in the Fall of 1907 and since then has hosted a dazzling array of luminaries, world leaders, and global entertainment stars. It has also been the site of many of the most important social occasions of this century and is Manhattan's premier hotel for weddings.

This is in large part due to the outstanding efforts of The Plaza's Executive Director of Catering, Lawrence D. Harvey, and his associates who have catered unforgettable events from small intimate brunches to Hollywood extravaganzas. In "A Plaza Wedding," Harvey offers Inspiration and Ideas for The Wedding of Your Dreams, covering every facet of planning the perfect wedding from engagement to reception. The book is lavishly illustrated with over 200 memorable full-color photos.

Like The Plaza, Fairmont is a name synonymous with luxury and impeccable service. We look forward to celebrating your wedding at each of our fine locations throughout the United States including: Chicago, Dallas, New Orleans, San Francisco, San Jose/Silicon Valley and now…The Plaza in New York.

Sincerely,

Robert I. Small

Robert I. Small

THE FAIRMONT HOTELS

AMERICA'S GRAND HOTELS SINCE 1907

WEDDING CAKE CREATED BY SYLVIA WEINSTOCK
FOR ALLISON LAMBERT AND HOWARD LUTNICK.

Preface

*I*n New York, when you think of weddings, you inevitably think of the Plaza. The hotel stands as a symbol of timeless elegance and graciousness that is unmatched in a city known for its landmarks.

Designed to replicate the Renaissance style of French châteaus, the Plaza rises in stately grandeur at the junction of Manhattan's most glamorous avenue and its most famous park, reflecting the glories of both. Inside, no detail has been overlooked—from the opulent rooms, to their unique appointments, to the attentiveness of the staff. The Plaza has a style all its own that has made it *the* place for weddings in New York, a tradition carried forward by successive generations of brides and grooms.

An extensive career as executive director of catering at premier hotels has made me a connoisseur of nuptials—from small, intimate brunches to fairy-tale productions. Together with a peerless, hand-picked staff, I've helped produce some of the most memorable weddings of the last three decades. Whether a wedding is to be simple and elegant or a gala—there are things that need to be done, in a specific order, with a reasonable amount of lead time.

This book is the harvest of years of meeting with brides-to-be to discuss wedding plans. Some arrive with a clear picture of their dream wedding, some know only what they *don't* want. No matter. Every bride wants a wedding that is significant, one that reflects how she feels about getting married—and one that will be happily remembered throughout her life.

A Plaza Wedding has been created to show how it is done, from the engagement to the grand finale.

Weddings are universal in nature—and unique in execution. To convey that is the aim of this book.

Lawrence D. Harvey
Executive Director of Catering, the Plaza Hotel

Foreword

What is it about the Plaza that makes it unique? The towering facade is palatial and imposing. Donald Trump's opulent restoration creates the sort of grandeur found in stately homes.

For a bride, having a wedding fete at the Plaza is the ultimate fantasy turned into reality. On her special day she ascends the portico steps with her retinue of bridesmaids, family, and friends. Hordes of well-wishers greet her throughout the hotel. The mood is set as she sweeps by the Palm Court with its beautiful flowers and salon music. Wherever she is headed—the Terrace Room, the Grand Ballroom, or one of the many beautiful suites—she is surrounded by an atmosphere steeped in romance and luxury. This is the Plaza.

As is Claridges in London, the Ritz in Madrid, the Beau Rivage in Lausanne, the Hassler in Rome, and the George V in Paris, the Plaza is New York's crown jewel. From 1907, when the Grand Ballroom made its debut, to the present day, the Plaza remains unique and unrivaled. Heads of state, society and business leaders, celebrities and the like from around the world— with such names as Eisenhower, Kennedy, Carnegie, Rockefeller, and the Princess Yasmin Aga Khan—have been a part of Plaza weddings. On each occasion, the setting was transformed by consummate designers into an original and wondrous decor.

What is it about the Plaza? For me, it is style, service, ambience, and quality coming together. Even when my morning paper seems to overflow with news of crises, disasters, and insurmountable problems, I can take refuge in a description of a wedding at the Plaza, where glamor, style, and taste will always have a place. Perhaps at this very moment, some bride and groom are celebrating the most memorable day of their lives at New York's most memorable institution—the Plaza Hotel.

CLIVE DAVID
Clive David Party Enterprises, Ltd.
Beverly Hills, California

Acknowledgments

I thank my lovely wife, Donna, for thirty-five wonderful years of marriage and for her steadfast encouragement to undertake this project, as well as our marvelous daughters Pam (Mrs. Gerald R. Taylor III) and Susan (Mrs. Darin Ramey), and our grandchildren, Gerald R. "Jason" Taylor IV, Zachary Alexander Ramey, Hunter Lawrence Campbell Ramey, and Courtney Nicole Taylor. Heartfelt thanks to my mother, Mrs. (Jean) Walter Neal, who has always believed that I could conquer the world. I thank Donald J. Trump. His leadership, vision, and commitment to the restoration of the Plaza and his standards of excellence in management have made this magnificent hotel the best in North America.

I thank my extraordinary staff, who helped make these fantastic weddings happen: William DeSaulnier, director of catering; Richard Pizzuto, assistant director of catering; Alex Miljkovic, executive catering manager; Linda Miller, catering manager; Robin Richards-Swan, catering manager; the incomparable Paul Nicaj, executive director of banquets, who, after twenty-four years here, is known as "Mr. Plaza"; Randy Janis, maître d'hôtel; and Bill Kennedy, assistant headwaiter.

A tremendous round of applause goes to executive chef Bruno Tison and his extraordinary staff of chefs for all their help with the menu composition and food photography for the book.

Special accolades to Asaad M. Farag, executive director of food and beverages; Joseph Friel, banquet chef; Eric Gouteyron, pastry chef; Martin Gilligan, chef garde-manger; Peter Fischl, Edwardian Room chef; Florimond Smoor, Oak Room chef; Edward Bitterly, Palm Court chef; and Peter Sherlock, executive sous chef.

Lou Manna, who produced the magnificent food photography, was a joy and delight to work with and a true professional. He was most ably assisted by Monica Baig, prop stylist; Laura Fasulka, assistant prop stylist; and Joan O'Brien, Bob La Mantia, and Stephen Bredin, photographer's assistants. Thanks also to Kal Barson for the financial section, which should be extremely helpful to young couples.

Pat Kerr and her sister Jana Edwards deserve extra special thanks for creating the jacket shot, as do models Valerie Marsch, Hillary K. Edwards, and Jason Taylor, and photographer Wendi Schneider.

Very special thanks to Jane Vitiello, who did much of the research and writing. Her help has been the backbone of the project.

I join John Grisham in praising the late Jay Garon of Jay Garon–Brooke Agency, our mutual literary agent, who believed in the project from day one and made it all happen. I'd like to salute as well Nancy Coffey, a very special person who helped pull the entire project together and held my hand along the way.

A special note of recognition goes to Tom Civitano, executive vice president of marketing, and Jacques Van Seters, managing director of the Plaza, and all Fairmont Executive Officers. A note of extra special thanks goes to my old friend Paul Von Ringelheim, who helped me lure Jay Garon and advised me on many aspects; to my dear friend Andy Marcus, who had the gargantuan task of assembling the photography; and to Sylvia Weinstock, the ultimate cake designer par excellence, and her talented husband, Ben. Thanks also to Gail Perl and Carol Berliner of Perl & Berliner. Special thanks to Harriette Rose Katz and to Barbara Feldman, bridal consultants, who contributed so much from their vast experience.

The incomparable Clive David of Clive David Party Enterprises, Ltd. of Beverly Hills, California, wrote the foreword of the book. Clive is a very special friend with whom I had the pleasure of doing the Pat Kluge fortieth birthday party and Perri Peltz's wedding. He is the consummate professional. Carol Horn contributed the tabletop section, and graphic designer Ellen Weldon was enormously helpful about invitation design. Thanks to musicians Hank Lane of the Hank Lane Orchestra (the official orchestra of the Plaza); Jerry Kravat of Jerry Kravat Entertainment; Alex Donner of Alex Donner Orchestra; Mark Stevens and Michael Carney of Michael Carney Music; Bob Hardwick of Bob Hardwick Sound; and Mark Stevens and his wife, Valerie Romanoff, of the Starlight Orchestra. Thanks to floral designers Philip Baloun of Philip Baloun Designs, who created the Lindenbaum decor; Larry and Elliott Atlas of Atlas Floral Decorators (official florist of the Plaza), who created the Donald Trump and Marla Maples decor; Michael and Denise Oppizi of Michael Oppizi & Co.; Anthony Ferraz, who created the Eddie Murphy decor, as well as the Lambert/Lutnick decor; and Stephen Kolens of Atlas Floral, who created the Silverman/Hodes decor. Thanks to photographers Sarah Merians, Harold Hechler, Mary Hilliard, and Denis Reggie, who made lovely contributions to the book. Also to Bert Leventhal of Newman and Leventhal Caterers, who created the elegant kosher menu for the Silverman wedding; and to the incomparable Chen Sam, who helped with the

Trump/Maples wedding. Extra special thanks to my assistant, Wendy Kligman, who was invaluable. Curt Gathje, manager of the office of the president at the Plaza, has been most helpful to me with many research items.

Special thanks to Steve Pagano for assisting with the write-up of the Lambert/Lutnick wedding. Andrew Krauss, assistant editor of Villard Books, was wonderful to work with, as was everyone at Villard. A very special person, Kerry White of Eddie Murphy Productions, made all the arrangements for the Nicole Mitchell and Eddie Murphy section. Janie Elder made all the arrangements for the Donald Trump and Marla Maples section. Both were a delight to work with. And thanks to all the wedding couples highlighted in the book.

Special accolades to:

- Mrs. Samuel Lindenbaum (Laurie Ellen Lindenbaum and Robert Allan Horne)
- Mrs. Laurence Cresci (Elisa Cresci and Timothy McEvoy)
- Dr. and Mrs. Charles Straniero (Carla Straniero and Dr. Robert Barone)
- Mrs. John J. Veronis (Perri Peltz and Eric Ruttenberg)
- Mrs. Jay Feinberg (Lisa Feinberg and Eric Blumencranz)
- Lisa Aitken and Dr. David Desmond
- Mr. and Mrs. Howard Silverman (Karen Jill Silverman and Dr. Leon Hodes)
- Donald J. Trump and Marla Maples
- Eddie Murphy and Nicole Mitchell
- Martha Kramer and Neal Jay Fox
- Allison Lambert and Howard Lutnick

And the many other brides and grooms who contributed to the book.

It has been an absolute delight to nurse this project from its inception to the completed book. I have made many new friends in the process and learned a lot about publishing. Best of all, I am able to leave to posterity an account of *A Plaza Wedding* in all its magnificence. In the years to come, I hope it will help many new brides and their mothers plan weddings with style, elegance, and flair. I thank each and every person who made a contribution to this project, including those inadvertently not mentioned.

This has been a labor of love.

LAWRENCE D. HARVEY

Contents

Opposite: Denis Reggie

A Plaza Wedding

Sometimes if they are having this enormous affair

in the Grand Ballroom I get there early to help Joe

set up the lights in the ceiling and before anybody gets

there we just scamper up this ladder and hide up there

in those holes

Oh my Lord is it ever swelteringly hot up there

I always wear my sun visor

Planning Ahead

With so much hope and promise invested in a marriage, it stands to reason that you want your wedding—the starting event, so to speak—to come off flawlessly. I can tell you one thing with certainty: Beautiful weddings don't just happen, they are the result of thoughtful planning and good organization. To have a faultless, unforgettable event, you must begin with an overall sense of what you want, have a firm grasp of priorities, and maintain a rigorous attention to detail throughout.

And what a welter of detail. Every wedding, no matter the scope, shares common elements. Whether your dream wedding is a simple, small-scale intimate gathering, a formal celebration rich in tradition, or a pull-out-all-the-stops extravaganza, some things remain the

FOR THE WEDDING OF LAURIE ELLEN LINDENBAUM AND ROBERT ALLAN HORNE, DESIGNER PHILIP BALOUN DECORATED THE CEILING WITH SIMILAX GARLANDS AND FESTOONS OF WHITE CHIFFON.

HAROLD HECHLER

THE PLAZA CHEFS.

same. You have to settle on a date and time. You have to select your sites and reserve them. Arrangements for the ceremony must be made. Guest lists have to be compiled, invitations issued, responses noted. Provisions must be made for receiving and acknowledging wedding gifts. You have to decide what sort of hospitality and atmosphere you wish to offer the guests who will be sharing your special day.

It goes without saying that the more elaborate the wedding celebration, the more lead time is needed, particularly if you have your heart set on certain elements. If there is to be a bridal party the participants must be asked and all the attendant details worked out. There are menus to be chosen, a wedding cake to order, and questions of overall decor and flowers to be decided. Music, photography, and videography all need to be arranged. And that's just the beginning. . . .

It takes at least six months to a year to plan a formal wedding—three to six months to plan an informal one. If enough time isn't left, you will find yourself having to settle for second or third choices—or simply what's available— rather than enjoying the wedding of your dreams. Even if you plan to hire a wedding consultant (and they are experts at seeing to it that what you want is what you get), they can only help you save time, not eliminate the need for it.

Nothing should be left to chance. Taking control of your wedding from the beginning and maintaining it throughout will insure that in the end it reflects your tastes and your intentions.

The Engagement

*I*t is only courteous to inform relatives and close friends of an engagement in person, by telephone, or with a handwritten note. A newspaper announcement is aimed at acquaintances and is therefore too impersonal, and engraved announcements are considered to be in poor taste. Two to three months before the wedding is the custom, although announcements may properly be sent anywhere from a year to a week ahead.

ANNOUNCING THE ENGAGEMENT

If there has been a recent death in the family or a family member is seriously ill, public announcements are not in good taste and should be delayed. Under no circumstances should an engagement be announced if a divorce or annulment is not final and one of the parties is still legally married to someone else.

The announcement is always made in the name of the bride's parents or her immediate family. If the groom's parents do not live in the same area as the bride's, they should be asked whether they would like to have the announcement appear in their local papers. If they would, the bride's mother sends a duplicate announcement to the papers they specify. In the absence of such an offer, the groom's mother may properly place such an announcement, but again, it is made in the name of the bride's parents.

JILL SCHWARTZBERG
AND DENNIS SHIELDS

SARAH MERIANS

*The pleasure of your company is requested
for cocktails and dinner
in honor of
Allison and Howard
on Thursday, the eighth of December
at half after seven o'clock
The Metropolitan Museum of Art
New York*

RSVP
Steven D. Pagano
(212) 938-3557

Business Attire
*Please use the museum's main
entrance at Fifth Ave & 82nd St.*

Lead times may vary depending on each particular newspaper, although four to six weeks is generally safe with large dailies and ten days with local weeklies. In most cases the announcement can be sent to the society editor. If you wish a photo to appear, it should accompany the announcement. A sharp, glossy, black-and-white print (of the bride alone or the couple) is best.

You can get a sense of how your announcement should be worded by looking at those previously printed. The basic format is:

Mr. and Mrs. [bride's parents] of [city, state, and second residence] announce the engagement of their daughter [bride's full name] to [groom's full name], son of [groom's parents] of [city, state, and second residence]. A [month] wedding is planned.

Miss [bride] attended/was graduated from [school or schools] and is [job title and employer]. Mr. [groom] attended/was graduated from [school or schools]. He is [job title and employer].

Circumstances may dictate some variations:

Mr./Mrs. [bride's surviving parent or custodial parent] of . . . announces the engagement of his/her daughter . . . to [groom, etc.]. Miss [bride's last name] is also the daughter of the late [deceased parent's full name]. Or . . . is also the daughter of [other parent] of [city, state].

. . . son of [surviving parent or custodial parent] and the late . . . Or . . . is also the son of [other parent] of . . .

Mr. and Mrs. [bride's remarried parent] announce . . . Miss [bride's last name] is also the daughter of . . .

If the bride is a young widow or divorcée, her parents can announce the engagement in the same manner they did the first time, using whatever surname their daughter actually uses.

FRED MARCUS

THE ENGAGEMENT PARTY

Although it is customary for the parents of the bride to give the engagement party, circumstances may be such that this is impractical. It is perfectly acceptable for the groom's parents to host an engagement party—or, in the absence of parents able to do so, any close relative. Where there has been a previous marriage and there are adult children, a very gracious and supportive gesture is for those children to give an engagement party in the couple's honor. Whatever the arrangement, *both* members of the engaged couple must be present. If this is not possible at the time of the announcement—if one is overseas, for instance—the party must be postponed until his or her return.

Invitations, formal printed ones or informal handwritten notes, may be sent or invitation may be made by telephone. If the bride's parents are giving the party, the invitations should be sent out in their name.

Toasts: The engagement is considered official when the father of the bride proposes a toast to her (the groom is included in his good wishes). Everyone rises but the engaged couple. Once the guests have toasted them, the groom rises to reply to the toast. If other members of the party wish to do so, they may propose toasts after the groom's reply.

ENGAGEMENT GIFTS

Engagement gifts are usually given to the bride only by relatives and close friends. Since others are not expected to do so, gifts should not be brought to the engagement party. The presents may be personal ones for the bride's use alone or items for her linen trousseau.

Gifts delivered in person may be acknowledged at the time—those that are sent should be immediately acknowledged with a note of thanks.

Although it is not necessary, should the bride-to-be choose to give her fiancé an engagement present, jewelry is generally considered to be appropriate.

Opposite: STEVEN LEBER,
FATHER OF BRIDE
MICHELLE LEBER ROBERTS.

Choosing a Date

Virtually the first decision you must make is when to hold your wedding. It is critical to choose a date that allows enough time for you to have the wedding you've set your heart on—at least six months to a year for a formal affair, a minimum of three to six months for something less elaborate.

Check a calendar to make sure that secular and religious holidays pose no problems. People are often unavailable during traditional family holidays such as Thanksgiving and Christmas. Also, take stock of how many of your guests will have to travel to your wedding. Out-of-town guests may appreciate ceremonies held on three-day weekends; hometown guests may not wish to give up their own getaway plans. If you are not having a civil ceremony, check your selected date against a religious calendar. There may be particular times during the year

Left: CARLA STRANIERO AND DR. ROBERT BARONE TOOK ADVANTAGE OF SPRING WEATHER WHEN THEY PLANNED THEIR ROMANTIC ARRIVAL AT THE PLAZA.

Below: CARLA STRANIERO BARONE AND HER BRIDESMAIDS.

when weddings may not be performed. And if you have your heart set on being married by a particular clergy member, be sure to check his or her availability as soon as you know your date.

You should always consider other family members' special occasions: Conflicting celebrations can result in wounded feelings or an unseemly tug-of-war for guests.

Remember that if you plan to hold your wedding in the peak seasons—October through December and April through June—booking the sites for the ceremony and reception will be more difficult (not to mention substantially more expensive) and you will find yourself competing for the services of the floral designer, musicians, and photographer, among others, of your choice. There are many advantages to having your wedding during the non-peak seasons; for starters, prices for the reception can drop by as much as 20 to 30 percent.

Time of day may be dictated by several things: the style of the wedding you desire, financial considerations, or, in the case of weekend Jewish weddings, by the Jewish Sabbath. A small intimate celebration can take the form of a wedding brunch, a sit-down luncheon, an afternoon tea dance, or a late-night supper, whereas formal weddings take place during the afternoon or evening. Bear in mind that costs tend to rise as the day progresses.

Above: MARLA MAPLES AND DONALD TRUMP CELEBRATED THE SEASON WITH A "WINTER WONDERLAND" THEME.

Left: ELISA CRESCI CHOSE BLACK AND WHITE AND DEEP RED ROSE BOUQUETS TO GIVE HER ATTENDANTS A VIVID SEASONAL LOOK.

ANTHONY FERRAZ'S MAGNIFICENT TENTED
CEILING IN A SUNBURST DESIGN OF WHITE
CHIFFON, FOR THE WEDDING OF ALLISON
LAMBERT AND HOWARD LUTNICK.

A Question of Style

Times may have changed, but a lot of young girls still dream of their wedding day with the same breathless anticipation as did their mothers and grandmothers. It isn't difficult to understand. The fairy-tale quality of a formal wedding can easily stir the imagination of a young girl to picture herself in the bride's place.

Not surprisingly, many brides-to-be have a clear sense of the sort of wedding they want. It is usually an amalgam of childhood impressions and details from every movie wedding they've ever seen, lovingly augmented through the years by their own tastes and preferences.

For those who never gave the question much thought, there are magazines and books that illustrate and describe a variety of wedding styles. A survey of friends and relatives can net useful ideas and suggestions.

Weddings fall into essentially three categories: formal, semiformal, and informal. While there are no hard-and-fast rules about what must be included—or excluded—in each, this is what is generally expected:

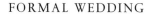

HAROLD HECHLER

ROBERT ALLAN
HORNE AND LAURIE
ELLEN LINDENBAUM

FORMAL WEDDING

Engraved invitations

two hundred or more guests

traditional ceremony

long white bridal gown with train and veil, if desired

long bridesmaids' dresses

tailcoats or cutaways for groom and attendants

maid and/or matron of honor, four or more bridesmaids, flower girl, ring bearer

best man, one usher per fifty guests or same number as bridesmaids

sit-down dinner

wedding cake

elaborate floral decorations and accessories (aisle carpet, pew ribbons, rose petals or confetti, limousines for bridal party, groom's cake, mementos)

music for ceremony, live music and/or disc jockey for dancing

SEMIFORMAL WEDDING

Engraved invitations

seventy-five to two hundred guests

traditional ceremony

long white bridal gown with veil, if desired

long bridesmaid's dresses

tuxedos for groom and attendants

maid and/or matron of honor, two to six bridesmaids, flower girl, ring bearer

best man, one usher per fifty guests or same number as bridesmaids

buffet (with or without bridal table and parents' tables)

wedding cake

extensive floral decorations and some accessories

music for ceremony, live music and/or disc jockey for dancing

INFORMAL WEDDING

Printed or handwritten invitations

seventy-five guests or fewer

simple ceremony

white or pastel cocktail dress, afternoon dress, cocktail suit, or simple long dress

similar attire for maid or matron of honor

dark suits for groom and best man

buffet (hors d'oeuvres and/or meal)

wedding cake

simple floral arrangements

music for ceremony and reception, optional

FRED MARCUS

MARY HILLIARD

Above: MARTHA KRAMER AND NEAL JAY FOX EXCHANGED VOWS BEFORE A GILDED FIREPLACE BANKED WITH PEONIES, ORCHIDS, ROSES, TULIPS, AND LILIES OF THE VALLEY DESIGNED BY FLORAL DECORATOR RINALDO MAIA.

Left: AN ELEGANT WEDDING LUNCHEON FOR SUSAN HARVEY AND DARIN RAMEY

Wedding Costs

Regardless of what style wedding you set your heart on, one of your first tasks is to determine what is affordable. For effective planning, a realistic overall budget is essential.

One useful way to decide what style wedding to have is to begin with your dream wedding. Picture it to yourself, then break that picture down into its essential components and list them:

- Size (approximate number of guests)
- Type (formal, semiformal, informal)
- Ceremony
- Type of reception
- Ambience (season, setting, decor, flowers)
- Bridal attire and bridal party
- Music
- Wedding cake

If you can't picture things, look at wedding books and bridal magazines to get some ideas. Once you know, more or less, what you are looking for, decide which aspects are really important to you, which are less critical, and which are expendable.

For instance, you may decide that rather than pare down your guest list, you prefer to simplify your arrangements. Or you may wish to share the best of everything with a smaller group of family and friends. If music and dancing are all-important to you and the bridal gown is just a dress you'll wear once—buy something simple and becoming to wear and hire the best band you can.

Sorting out your priorities right from the start will help you apportion your total budget in the way that is the most meaningful to you. The next step is to begin making appointments to find out what is available, what it will cost, and whether it will fit your budget.

Luckily, wedding options are almost limitless. Even if you have to modify, pare down, or eliminate some components, you would be surprised how much of the essence of your dream wedding you can retain with proper professional advice.

Choosing the right people to work with can make all the difference. No matter what style wedding you ultimately select, they can help you make it the very best of its kind.

Preparing a Wedding Budget

ITEM	COST	ITEM	COST
ENGAGEMENT PARTY		*BRIDE'S GIFTS FOR ATTENDANTS*	
STATIONERY, ETC.		*GROOM'S GIFTS FOR ATTENDANTS*	
Invitations/enclosures		*ACCOMMODATIONS*	
Stationery		Bridesmaids	
Announcements		Groomsmen	
Postage		Visiting clergy member	
CEREMONY		*TRANSPORTATION*	
Site/facility fee		Bridal party	
Clergy member's fee		Others	
Blood tests		*FLOWERS AND DECOR*	
Marriage license		Lighting, ceremony	
ATTIRE		Lighting, reception	
Bride's gown		Draperies, ceremony	
Headpiece and veil		Draperies, reception	
Accessories		Carpeting, ceremony	
Hairdresser		Carpeting, reception	
Makeup artist		Linens, reception	
Manicurist		Flowers, ceremony	
Dresser		Flowers, reception	
Bride's attendants		Bride's bouquet	
Groom's formal wear		Flowers for bride's attendants	
Groom's attendants		Boutonnieres	
Flower girl		Corsages	
Ring bearer		*MUSIC*	
BRIDESMAID'S LUNCHEON		Engagement party	
BACHELOR'S DINNER		Ceremony	
REHEARSAL DINNER		Reception	
BRIDE'S RING			
GROOM'S RING			

ITEM	COST	ITEM	COST
PHOTOGRAPHY		*RECEPTION*	
Engagement party		Per person	
Ceremony		Liquor/bar	
Reception		Equipment	
VIDEOGRAPHY		Gratuities	
Engagement party		*WEDDING CAKE*	
Ceremony			
Reception		**TOTAL COST**	

Left: MARLA MAPLES AND DONALD TRUMP WALKED DOWN AN AISLE
BORDERED BY WHITE BALUSTRADES OF SIMILAX VINES AND WHITE
ORCHIDS—THE CREATION OF LARRY ATLAS.

Right: FOR THE WEDDING OF PERRI PELTZ AND ERIC RUTTENBERG
EACH TIER OF SYLVIA WEINSTOCK'S CAKE WAS NEARLY A FOOT HIGH
AND HAD LACE ICING SURROUNDED BY BASKETS OF SPUN SUGAR
ROSES, LILY OF THE VALLEY, AND PALE GREEN HYDRANGEA.

*T*he lists that follow represent the traditional division of wedding expenses. The lists are comprehensive, but they are in no way meant to imply that every item is essential. Concentrate on the elements you think you will want or need and make your own list. For the moment, disregard the rest.

THE BRIDE AND HER FAMILY

- Fee for a bridal consultant
- Invitations, announcements, enclosures, stationery
- Wedding dress, headpiece, veil, and accessories
- Trousseau and lingerie
- Rental fee for ceremony site
- Fee for sexton or caretaker of temple
- Bride's bouquet (in some areas the groom pays)
- Bouquets, corsages for attendants
- Flowers and decor (special lighting, draperies, table linens, carpeting, etc.) for ceremony and reception
- Photography
- Videography
- Music for ceremony and reception
- Transportation for bridal party to ceremony and reception
- Wedding reception
- Gratuities
- Gifts for bride's attendants
- Gift for groom
- Groom's wedding ring
- Transportation and accommodations for out-of-town clergy member (if invited to perform ceremony by bride's family)
- Accommodations for bride's attendants
- Bridesmaids' luncheon

THE GROOM AND HIS FAMILY

- Bride's engagement and wedding rings
- Bride's wedding present
- Marriage license
- Blood tests
- Fee for officiating clergy member
- Transportation and accommodations for out-of-town clergy member (if invited to perform ceremony by groom's family)
- Rehearsal dinner
- Bachelor dinner*
- Transportation and accommodations for groom's parents
- Honeymoon
- Transportation for groom and best man to ceremony
- Bride's bouquet (where custom demands it), going-away corsage
- Corsages for immediate family members (bride's and groom's)
- Gifts for groom's attendants
- Accommodations for groom's attendants
- Boutonnieres for groom's attendants
- Ties and gloves for groom's attendants

* May be given by groom or groomsmen.

BRIDE'S ATTENDANTS

- Bridesmaid's dress and accessories
- Personal traveling expenses
- Wedding gift (contribution to joint bridesmaids' gift or individual gift to couple)
- Wedding shower or luncheon for the bride

OUT-OF-TOWN GUESTS

- Personal traveling and lodging expenses

GROOM'S ATTENDANTS

- Wedding attire
- Personal traveling expenses
- Wedding gift (contribution to joint groom's gift or individual gift to couple)
- Bachelor dinner[†]

Except for variations of ethnic or local custom, this is the *traditional* division of expenses. Nowadays, circumstances may call for other perfectly acceptable variations:

- The bride and groom may choose to pay their wedding costs.
- The groom's family may offer to pay a share.

- The groom's family may offer to pay for additional guests of theirs.
- The groom's family may offer to pay for particular items such as liquor or music.

Although there is nothing insulting or improper about the groom's family offering to share expenses, it is not proper for the bride's family to ask. If the budget is limited but no offer is made, the bride's family should proceed with whatever wedding arrangements they feel they can comfortably afford.

[†]*May be given by groom or groomsmen.*

FRED MARCUS

THE STRIKING CONTRAST OF
BLACK VELVET AGAINST WHITE
LENT A HEIGHTENED DRAMA
TO ELISA CRESCI'S
ATTENDANTS' GOWNS.

DENIS GARTNER

Wedding Consultants

*I*n times gone by, the services of a social secretary were a luxury enjoyed by a rather select few. (No doubt those services were highly prized when it came to giving a family wedding.) Today one needn't be a society matron with a debutante daughter to have access to such professional help.

If you are planning a large formal wedding with two hundred or more guests, if your aims are modest but you aren't able to devote the time needed to do the legwork and follow up on details, if you prefer to make the decisions and have someone else do the actual work—consider a bridal consultant.

The advantages to engaging a consultant are numerous:

∞ **You have access to someone with very specialized knowledge and experience.**

∞ **You don't have to worry about learning from your mistakes; you're dealing with a professional who wouldn't be in business long if she or he made mistakes.**

∞ **You're less apt to find yourself feeling overwhelmed as the wedding date approaches.**

∞ **The burden of seeing to it that everything is as it should be is not yours alone.**

Engaging a bridal consultant does *not* mean someone else is making the decisions—it means someone else is doing most of the work. The best way to find a good consultant is to ask for names from people whose weddings you've admired or whose taste and judgment you trust. Then meet with the consultant. Remember: You're looking for an ally—someone prepared to act as your intermediary on every aspect of your wedding, someone alert to the niceties and fine points that make a wedding look special, someone who can troubleshoot beforehand and make certain everything is under control on the day of the event.

If you have an aptitude for organizing large-scale events and enjoy looking after details yourself, there is no reason why you shouldn't do so. Whether you hire a bridal consultant to help you or you choose to oversee and carry out every task yourself, the decisions remain yours.

Opposite: FROM THE WEDDING
OF LISA FEINBERG AND
ERIC BLUMENCRANZ

Bride's Timetable

ONE YEAR TO SIX MONTHS IN ADVANCE

Decide style of wedding ceremony and reception

Select date and time of day

Hire bridal consultant (optional)

Decide location for ceremony and reception; reserve both

Confirm availability of person officiating

Decide on number of guests

Decide on bridal party and ask them to serve

Order invitations, enclosures, announcements, and stationery

SIX MONTHS TO THREE MONTHS IN ADVANCE

If you are having a religious ceremony, meet with clergy member to discuss details and procedures

Select and order bridal gown; arrange for fittings

Select and order attendants' gowns; arrange for fittings

Prepare guest lists

Hire floral designer

Book musicians and/or disc jockey

Select photographer and videographer

Select baker for wedding cake

TWO MONTHS IN ADVANCE

Arrange for the bridal party's transportation to the ceremony and reception

Decide on dinner service, silver, and stemware patterns and list selections for bridal registry

Above: GUESTS AT THE WEDDING OF ELISA CRESCI AND TIM McEVOY TRAVELED FROM THE CHURCH CEREMONY TO THE PLAZA BY CHARTERED BUS.

Left: PERFORMING AT THE RECEPTION FOR MARLA MAPLES AND DONALD TRUMP, MARK STEVENS OF THE HANK LANE ORCHESTRA.

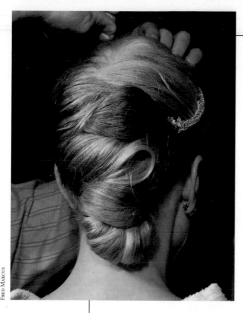

FRED MARCUS

MARLA MAPLES'S
INTRICATE CHIGNON WAS
THE CREATION OF
FREDERICK FEKKAI OF THE
FREDERICK FEKKAI
BEAUTY CENTER AT
BERGDORF GOODMAN.

Check on fittings and accessories for attendants

Finalize selection of linens, draperies, lighting scheme, floral arrangements, bouquets, and so forth with floral designer

Select music for ceremony and reception

Work out details and arrangements with photographer and videographer

Finalize menu and other arrangements for reception

Decide on wedding cake flavor and style

See hairdresser to try out style for wedding

See makeup artist for consultation

Select wedding rings

Collect information on accommodations for out-of-town guests (reserve block of rooms if necessary)

Arrange for housing of out-of-town attendants

Address and stuff invitations

Mail invitations six weeks before wedding date

Check to make certain groom and groomsmen have arranged for formal wear

ONE MONTH IN ADVANCE

Arrange for blood tests and marriage license

Record gifts; write thank you notes

Decide on honeymoon clothing

Double-check on bridal and attendants' accessories

Make final arrangements with floral designer, musicians, wedding cake baker, banquet manager, photographer, videographer, etc.

If taking groom's last name, arrange for name change on pertinent documents

Arrange for bridesmaids' luncheon

Address and stamp announcements for mailing the day after wedding

Make out seating plan for bridal party and parents' tables

Work out tentative seating plan for guests

Send wedding announcement to newspapers

Arrange for wedding rehearsal, rehearsal dinner; notify bridal party

Make hair, makeup, manicure, and pedicure appointments

TWO WEEKS IN ADVANCE

Confirm all lodging arrangements

Confirm details with floral designer, banquet manager, and others

ONE WEEK IN ADVANCE

Buy gifts for attendants

Buy gift for groom

Give final guest count to banquet manager

ONE OR TWO DAYS IN ADVANCE

Have manicure, pedicure

WEDDING DAY—MORNING

Have hair done

Check on any orders not being delivered to
see that they've been picked up

TWO HOURS BEFORE CEREMONY

Dresser and/or attendants to arrive wherever
you are dressing

ONE HOUR BEFORE CEREMONY

Have makeup done

Dress

Ushers arrive at place of ceremony

ONE HALF HOUR BEFORE CEREMONY

Groom and best man arrive at place of
ceremony

Background music begins

Guests begin arriving and are seated

Best man checks last-minute arrangements
and gives officiating clergy or justice
honorarium

Family members and honored guests are
seated "within the ribbon" or in pews
near front

FIVE MINUTES BEFORE CEREMONY

Groom's parents arrive, mother is escorted to
her seat, followed by her husband*

Bride's mother is escorted to her seat in the
front row*

White carpet, or aisle runner, rolled down the
aisle

Bride's father takes his place with bride*

Attendants take their places in proper order
for processional

Music starts and ushers lead procession down
the aisle

*In Orthodox and Conservative Jewish wedding ceremonies, the
groom is escorted by both his parents, as is the bride.*

JANIE ELDER, MAID OF HONOR
TO MARLA MAPLES.

Master Checklist

Officiating clergy or justice of the peace ☐

Caterer ☐

Menu ☐

Wedding cake ☐

Liquor ☐

Flowers ☐

Music ☐

Invitations and stationery ☐

Bridal attire: bride, groom, attendants ☐

Wedding rings ☐

Photography ☐

Videography ☐

Newspaper announcements ☐

Bridal registry ☐

Marriage license and blood tests ☐

Name-change details (if required) ☐

Prewedding dinners or parties ☐

Rehearsal/rehearsal dinner ☐

Seating plans ☐

Attendants' gifts ☐

Out-of-town attendants and guests ☐

Transportation ☐

Trousseau ☐

Honeymoon plans ☐

Receiving line ☐

FRED MARCUS

Above: MICHELLE LEBER ROBERTS'S OFF-THE-SHOULDER FORMAL GOWN AND ELBOW-LENGTH VEIL

Right: WEDDING CAKE BY SYLVIA WEINSTOCK FOR THE WEDDING OF MARTHA KRAMER AND NEAL JAY FOX

MARY HILLIARD

Choosing Wedding Attendants

FROM THE WEDDING
OF MICHELLE LEBER
AND MICHAEL ROBERTS.

There are several considerations in choosing attendants for your wedding: affection for particular friends or relatives; a gracious gesture toward a groom's sibling; family obligations; an opportunity to include someone in whose wedding party you have served. Ultimately, the choice is yours.

You may invite as many or as few attendants as you wish, but if you are planning a large, formal wedding, four to six bridesmaids is usual. You may have more ushers than bridesmaids (if you plan to have one usher for every fifty guests), but not the reverse. While too large a bridal party can be unwieldy, you may wish to expand somewhat to accommodate young siblings or children from a previous marriage by having some junior bridesmaids and ushers along with a flower girl, ring bearer, or pages.

It is customary to ask your closest sister to be maid or matron of honor. If you are planning a relatively small wedding and you would like both your sister and your closest friend to be attendants, you may have a maid and a matron of honor. (In such a case, the maid of honor takes precedence.) Although it is not unusual for a groom's father to serve as best man, the bride's mother, as hostess of the wedding, does not serve as matron of honor.

Wedding attendants should be asked to serve as soon as a date has been chosen for the wedding. (Being asked is an honor that should not be refused for any but a very compelling reason.) In the event of a last-minute crisis, it is perfectly acceptable to ask a friend or relative to replace a bridesmaid who is unable to attend.

All members of the wedding party—as well as the parents of any small children who may be serving—are responsible for the costs of their wedding costumes.

The Bridal Party

THE MAID OR MATRON OF HONOR

The maid or matron of honor is aide and confidante to the bride, sharing as many prewedding chores as she can. If she is not a member of the bride's family, she generally gives a shower for the bride. On the wedding day, she sees to it that the attendants are dressed as they should be and, if there is no professional dresser, helps the bride with her dress.

The maid of honor precedes the bride and her father down the aisle. During the ceremony she holds the bride's bouquet, adjusts her veil, and arranges the train when the bride turns to leave the altar. The maid of honor is the witness by law and signs the marriage certificate. In the receiving line, the maid of honor stands next to the bridal couple, and at the bridal table, she sits on the groom's left. She also helps the bride on with her going-away clothes.

THE BEST MAN

Of all the attendants, the best man carries the greatest burden of duties and responsibilities. He coordinates the selection, purchase, and payment for the ushers' gift to the groom and makes the presentation at the rehearsal dinner. It is his job to help the groom pack for his honeymoon and to see to it that his going-away clothes are brought to the reception.

On the day of the wedding, the best man sees to it that the ushers are properly dressed and aware of the ceremony procedure. He makes certain the groom is dressed in plenty of time and takes charge of

Above: CARLA STRANIERO AND HER ATTENDANTS LEAVING FOR THE WEDDING.

Right: DONALD TRUMP WITH HIS BEST MAN—HIS FATHER, FRED TRUMP.

FRED MARCUS

THE USHERS

The groom's ushers are generally brothers, relatives, close friends, and brothers of the bride near in age to the groom. A head usher may be deputized to supervise the others and designate who is to escort members of the immediate family. (Brothers of the bride and groom who are ushers escort their own mothers; if there are none, the head usher may choose to do so.) The ushers' major responsibility is to see that family members and guests are seated where they wish.

While ushers are expected to pay the cost of their wedding clothes, their gloves, ties, and boutonnieres (if not included in their rental) are provided by the groom. If there is a bachelor dinner, ushers are included in the invitation. They also contribute to a joint gift for the groom.

THE JUNIOR USHERS

Like their female counterparts, junior ushers are boys too young to be regular ushers whom you nevertheless wish to include in the bridal party. Their only role is to be part of the processional.

THE RING BEARER

The ring bearer is a small boy between the ages of three and seven who carries the wedding ring on a white satin or velvet cushion. (The ring should be fixed to the cushion in such a way that it does not roll off while carried but is simple for the best man to remove at the point in the ceremony when he takes it.) The ring bearer traditionally wears a white—or, sometimes, navy—suit of short pants and an Eton jacket. Miniature tuxedos or cutaways are in poor taste.

THE PAGES

Pages should come in pairs as they are basically needed only if your gown has a cathedral train. Their sole duty is to carry the train during the processional and recessional.

Opposite Right: RINGBEARER HALEY ULLOA.
FROM THE WEDDING OF LOURDES TORRES
AND MARC RUBIN. *Opposite Left:* JASON
TAYLOR. FROM THE WEDDING OF SUSAN
HARVEY AND DARIN RAMEY.

Fred Marcus

Sarah Merians

Wedding Attire

THE BRIDE

Perhaps nothing says "wedding" quite so definitively as a white bridal gown and veil—for many, it is *the* signature element. Despite its associations, the pure white wedding costume is not a tradition from time immemorial, it was simply a fashion begun by Queen Victoria at her wedding in 1840. The fashion caught on and held: White indisputably remains the most popular choice for first-time brides. Nowadays the dictates of custom have relaxed sufficiently to make white or off-white an acceptable choice for second-time brides as well.

FRED MARCUS   DENIS GARTNER   FRED MARCUS

The origin of the veil is less certain. It appeared intermittently from Roman times on, but it only became a requisite of the bridal ensemble sometime in the nineteenth century. Unless religious custom demands one, veils are generally the province of young, first-time brides. A mature bride may wish to flout convention and wear a veil—a second-time bride should not, nor should she select a dress with a train.

Whether your tastes are simple or baroque, it is difficult to resist the lure of a wedding dress as an expression of your true self, your dream self, or some wonderful combination of both. Your wedding day is one of the few times in your life when you can give your imagination free rein—and find everyone, including perfect strangers, applauding your effort. A bride in her wedding costume is the cynosure of all eyes.

Personal tastes apart, your choice should also reflect the style of your wedding. Day or evening, formal weddings call for floor-length dresses in some shade of white or ivory. Fabrics such as satin, lace, or taffeta are well suited to the drape and sweep of very formal gowns. A cathedral (two and one-half yards) or chapel (one and one-third yards) train, a full-length veil secured by a headpiece, and gloves, if you like, complete the ensemble. (If your dress has a cap sleeve or is sleeveless, long gloves should be worn.)

A less formal version would be a floor-length gown with a chapel train in a somewhat less elaborate material than the very formal gown. The veil could be to the hem, fingertip length, or shoulder length.

Top: ALLISON LAMBERT LUTNICK'S HEADPIECE: A TIARA-SHAPED BAND ENCRUSTED WITH PEARLS. A FIVE-YARD-LONG TRAIN, SPRINKLED WITH CLUSTERS OF PEARLS AND SEQUINS, WAS LATER ATTACHED TO THE HEADPIECE.
Above: DEBORAH GALANT LAZAR'S RICHLY APPLIQUED FORMAL GOWN.

Opposite Left: ORA SCHORR KRIEGSTEIN IN A TRADITIONAL FORMAL GOWN WITH HEADPIECE AND VEIL. *Opposite Center:* LISA FEINBERG BLUMENCRANZ IN A ROMANTIC OFF-THE-SHOULDER FORMAL GOWN AND FINGERTIP VEIL. *Opposite Right:* THE CLEAN LINES AND CLASSIC SIMPLICITY OF SUSAN HARVEY RAMEY'S DRESS WERE PERFECT FOR AN ELEGANT WEDDING LUNCHEON.

FRED MARCUS

Above: BRIDAL FINERY FROM THE WEDDING OF ELISA CRESCI AND TIM McEVOY.

For a semiformal wedding, the dress can be long, tea length, or even short, with no train. The veil is elbow length or shorter.

For informal weddings, bridal costumes can range from simple but elegant long dresses, to cocktail dresses, to cocktail suits. White, or any color but black, is acceptable.

One may properly wear satin in all seasons, but weather and comfort should be a consideration when selecting the material for your dress. Organdy, tulle, fine cotton, and chiffon are all practical options for hot weather; brocades and velvets are lovely for winter weddings.

Headpieces used to secure the veil come in a variety of styles. The *floral wreath* is a circlet of flowers that can be worn on top of the head or around the forehead. The *Juliet cap*—ornamented as elaborately as you like—is a fitted skullcap worn at the back of the head. The *profile* is a cluster of fabric flowers, pearl sprays, or crystal sprays attached to a comb. It is worn on one side of the head, angled toward the face. Other options include the *mantilla,* which is generally made of lace, is secured to a lovely comb, and gently frames each side of the face; and the *chignon,* a cluster of flowers or pearl sprays worn at the back of the head. Hats such as picture hats or small pillboxes can be very becoming with the right costume.

Above all, choose something that is becoming to you. Wedding portraits are probably the most looked-at photographs during anyone's lifetime. Your bridal costume should make you look lovely and feel absolutely radiant.

THE BRIDESMAIDS

The considerations in choosing bridesmaids' dresses are more numerous than in choosing your own. The dresses should complement the wedding gown in style and degree of formality, the fabric and color should be appropriate to the season, the style and color should be flattering to all the bridesmaids, and the cost (unless a present is being made of the dresses) should be reasonable.

The bride may choose a dress without consulting anyone in the bridal party, or she may narrow choices down to two or three and leave the final choice to a consensus. Unless each of

FRED MARCUS

SLEEK LINES AND VIVID COLOR IN HER BRIDESMAIDS' GOWNS PROVIDED A COUNTERPOINT TO NICOLE MITCHELL MURPHY'S FORMAL GOWN.

Left: In addition to designing the bride's gown, Carolyne Roehm created this romantic look for Perri Peltz Ruttenberg's attendants and flower girls. The gowns complemented the elaborate decor of the formal "garden" wedding.

SARAH MERIANS

Above: LAUREN REIFF STERN WITH HER ATTENDANTS.

your attendants is similarly built and has the same coloring, pick a style that suits a range of figures. Equally, the color should be flattering to a range of complexions.

Pale pastels remain the shades of choice for spring and summer, jewel tones are popular for fall and winter, and black-and-white weddings are enjoying a current vogue. Bridesmaids may also wear white, but the style must be carefully chosen to harmonize with—not detract from—the bridal gown.

As a rule, bridesmaids' dresses are identical, as are their accessories. Shoes are purchased individually for the sake of fit, but should be as close in style as possible. If they need to be dyed to match dresses, they should all be done in one lot. The maid of honor's ensemble may be set apart by some variation in style or color that indicates her position as honor attendant.

Depending on their age, junior bridesmaids may wear the same dresses as the regular bridesmaids or a more youthful adaptation.

THE FLOWER GIRL

The flower girl may wear a dress made from the same fabric and in the same color as the bridesmaids' costumes—or a white dress, if the bride chooses. Whatever the material or color, the dress should be in a style becoming to a little girl, not a parody of an adult dress.

THE GROOM

Proper attire for the groom at a formal evening wedding offers little in the way of choice: black tailcoat, matching satin-trimmed trousers, stiff white shirt with a wing collar, white waistcoat, and a white tie. For a wedding scheduled before six o'clock, formal day clothes comprise a black or Oxford-gray cutaway with black or gray striped trousers, pearl-gray waistcoat, stiff white shirt, stiff fold-down collar, and black-and-gray four-in-hand or dress ascot.

For semiformal evening weddings, a black or midnight-blue dinner jacket is worn with a white piqué or pleated-front shirt with attached collar, black bow tie, and black waistcoat or cummerbund. In the warmth of the summer, a white dinner jacket is worn with a black cummerbund. Semiformal daytime weddings call for a black or dark gray sack coat, black or gray striped trousers, pearl-gray waistcoat, soft white shirt, and a black-and-gray four-in-hand.

Practical considerations usually discourage people from putting on formal daytime weddings in tropical climates or during the heat of the summer. Proper attire for informal weddings is a lightweight suit—or a navy or dark gray jacket paired with white trousers—white dress socks and white dress shoes, or black dress socks with black dress shoes. White jackets and dark gray trousers are also acceptable.

MARY HILLIARD

Above: FROM THE WEDDING OF MARTHA KRAMER AND NEAL JAY FOX.

Below: DR. DAVID DESMOND AND HIS GROOMSMEN.

FRED MARCUS

Uniformity is the look desired, but the groom and his best man may wear ties of a slightly different pattern than the remaining groomsmen, or ascots while they wear ties.

A groom who is a member of the armed forces may elect to wear his dress uniform in place of formal wear.

THE USHERS

The best man and ushers wear the same attire as the groom (with possible variations of tie or ascot for the groom and the best man). If possible, all the groomsmen's cutaways or tuxedos should be rented from the same place to insure that they will be identical. Providing gloves and ties—once the province of the groom's family—can generally be left to the rental agency, as can providing dress shoes.

If the groom and all his attendants are in the service, they may certainly wear their dress uniforms. However, having some ushers in dress uniforms and some in formal wear would spoil the look of the wedding party.

THE RING BEARER

A young ring bearer should wear either a white linen suit with short pants and an Eton jacket, white shoes, and white socks; or a navy suit with dark knee socks and black shoes.

THE BRIDE'S FATHER

The bride's father (or whoever is escorting her down the aisle) customarily wears the same attire as the groom and his attendants to maintain the uniformity of the bridal procession. The groom's father may do so as well, whether he is part of the procession or not.

FROM THE WEDDING OF NICOLE SILVER
AND BRAD SCHEFLER.

Wedding Rings

WITH THIS RING . . .

What was once offered as a token of good intentions (and security—a sort of down payment, if you will) is viewed more romantically nowadays as a token of love and commitment. For years, tradition had it that the man popped the question and produced the engagement ring in a virtually simultaneous action. Whether it was solemnly proffered or whipped out with a flourish (or hidden for the bride to discover in some antic scenario) depended, as did the style of the ring, on the temperament and taste of the groom.

FRED MARCUS

DESIGNED AND HAND-CRAFTED BY
THE HOUSE OF HARRY WINSTON

Times change. Engagement rings are certainly not required for becoming engaged, but the custom is widespread. Dramatic as a surprise presentation may be, consulting with one's fiancée—or having her select her ring—is both correct and considerate.

While the stone of choice remains the diamond, colored stones—particularly emeralds, sapphires, and rubies—have become increasingly popular. Some brides opt for their birthstone or the groom's birthstone.

BIRTHSTONES

JANUARY	Garnet
FEBRUARY	Amethyst
MARCH	Aquamarine, bloodstone
APRIL	Diamond
MAY	Emerald, agate
JUNE	Pearl
JULY	Ruby, onyx
AUGUST	Carnelian, peridot, sardonyx
SEPTEMBER	Sapphire
OCTOBER	Opal, beryl, moonstone
NOVEMBER	Topaz
DECEMBER	Turquoise

Wedding rings may be purchased as part of a matching engagement and wedding ring set or separately. If the latter, the element for the band is the same as in the engagement ring. If there is to be a double-ring ceremony, the bands should be well matched.

Bands range from simple circlets, to ornately carved or intertwined bands, to bands embellished with diamonds and other stones. It should be noted that Jewish custom demands the groom give, and the bride accept, some object of nominal value for a marriage to be legally binding. Since the seventh century the object has been a ring. In accordance with Jewish law, the ring must be *unpierced* and unadorned with stones. In addition, traditional rabbis do not perform double-ring ceremonies as they feel this invalidates the original dictum. Other rabbis may incorporate the bride's gift of a ring to the groom into the ceremony.

Mr. and Mrs. Howard Silverman

request the pleasure of your company

at the marriage of their daughter

Karen Jill

to

Dr. Leon Hodes

son of

Dr. and Mrs. Meyer Hodes

Saturday, the seventeenth of September

One thousand nine hundred and ninety-four

at half after seven o'clock

The Plaza

New York

Black tie

Invitations

The format and style of formal wedding invitations is almost as fixed as the changing of the guard at Buckingham Palace. In time-honored phrases engraved on suitably heavy white or ecru stock, the parents of the bride issue their invitation. While accommodations may be made to circumstance—divorce, remarriage, someone other than the bride's parents hosting the wedding—the wording remains essentially the same. The typeface is one of a handful of elegant script or Roman faces, and the overall look is unmistakable. Receipt of such an invitation cannot fail to signal a traditional formal wedding.

Of course, other options are available. Keeping in mind the size, scope, and style of your wedding, invitations can range from the whimsical to the ornate, depending on your budget

FRED MARCUS

and your inclination. The invitation described above is always correct (and it is certainly appropriate for a formal wedding), but nowadays one sees many creative variations—exotic papers in unusual shades, witty graphics, intricate folds. Whatever the choice, your invitation should complement the style of your wedding.

The most important thing to remember is that an invitation is intended to convey whatever information your guests will need to get to your wedding, and it should do so in the clearest, most gracious manner possible.

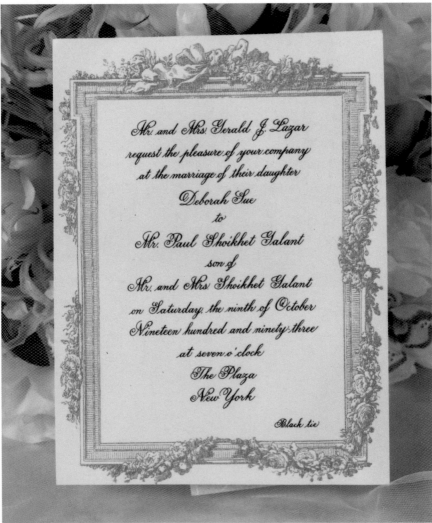

FRED MARCUS

ENGAGEMENT PARTY INVITATIONS

Engagement party invitations are sent out in the name of the bride's parents unless, for some reason, the groom's parents or other relatives or friends are hosting the party. The usual wording is:

Mr. and Mrs. Jordan Lee Ashton
request the pleasure of your company
at a dinner in honor of
Miss Haley Brett Ashton
and
Mr. Justin Scott Rohmer
Saturday, the tenth of January
at eight o'clock
895 Cherokee Place
New York City

INVITATION TO MEET YOU OR YOUR FIANCÉ

To meet
Miss Haley Brett Ashton

Mr. and Mrs. Peter Adam Rohmer
request the pleasure of your company
at a cocktail reception
Friday, the fifth of February
at seven o'clock
17 Chester Court
Cazenovia, New York

SAVE-THE-DATE CARDS

If you have planned a wedding on a traditional holiday weekend or during a holiday season, you may wish to take the precaution of sending your guests save-the-date cards to alert them to your plans. These should be sent at least three months in advance of the wedding. Save-the-date cards, which should match your wedding invitations, are printed on heavy card stock in white or ecru and are mailed in an envelope.

Please save the date of
Saturday, the third of July
for the wedding of
Miss Haley Brett Ashton
to
Mr. Justin Scott Rohmer
Invitation to follow

REHEARSAL DINNER INVITATIONS

Inasmuch as the rehearsal dinner is hosted by the groom's parents (as a courtesy to the bride's family), invitations emanate from them. The invitation style should be in keeping with the wedding invitation—but not matching. An engraved, flat white card is always tasteful. The wording may be formal or somewhat informal.

If the rehearsal dinner is small and reserved solely for members of the wedding party, it is perfectly acceptable for the groom's parents to write a simple invitation on their informals if they wish. If the rehearsal dinner is a more ambitious affair and includes out-of-town guests and others, an engraved invitation is more appropriate. In either case, the invitation should be mailed two weeks before the wedding.

Mr. and Mrs. Peter Adam Rohmer
request the pleasure of your company
at a rehearsal dinner
in honor of
Miss Haley Brett Ashton
and
Mr. Justin Scott Rohmer
Friday, the second of July
at half after eight o'clock
Café Raphael
New York City

or:

Peter and Daniele Rohmer
request the pleasure of your company
at a rehearsal dinner for
Haley and Justin
Friday, July second
at eight-thirty
Café Raphael
New York City

or, on the front of the informal:

Mr. and Mrs. Peter Adam Rohmer
Dinner, Friday, July 2 at 8:30
Café Raphael

and on the inside, handwritten:

Dear Carrie and Sam,
Peter and I hope you will join us for dinner
after
the rehearsal at the Café Raphael.
We look forward to seeing you.
Love,
Daniele

WEDDING INVITATIONS

There are several elements to wedding invitations that, combined, form the basis for assessing their quality. The first is paper. The finest paper is made from cotton and feels rich and luxurious to the touch. The heavier the paper, the more this tactile sense of quality is enhanced. Granted, a heavyweight paper made of 100 percent cotton is expensive. What should be considered, however, is that your invitation sets the tone for your wedding. No matter how well designed an invitation is, using less than a good quality paper inevitably detracts from its effect.

Formal invitations can be engraved on ecru (any of a number of shades of off-white including ivory, cream, eggshell, and buff) or white paper. Less traditional invitations may be done in a variety of shades.

Another element that determines a fine wedding invitation is the process by which the wording is reproduced. The most elegant wedding invitations are engraved, which means that the impression raises the paper itself and the ink adheres to the raised surface. If you turn over an engraved invitation you will see an indentation; no other reproduction process produces either this indentation or the distinctive ripple you can feel across the front. Thermography, a process that is less expensive than engraving, creates a similar sensation of raised print without the other distinguishing effects.

Formal invitations are generally—though not exclusively—engraved in black ink. If you intend to use a bold, fairly heavy typeface, you may wish to have the invitations engraved in some shade of dark gray rather than black so that the type does not appear overpowering.

Whether you opt for a Roman or script typeface is very much a matter of individual taste. What should be borne in mind is the need to select something that is not only aesthetically pleasing but readable. Heavily ornate typestyles or spidery lettering with lots of flourishes and curlicues can be difficult to decipher and can give the invitation a messy look.

FRED MARCUS

The traditional wedding invitation has a fold on the left-hand side so that the invitation opens like a book. You may choose a small letter sheet that folds once, or a larger letter sheet that is folded a second time to go into the envelope. Sheets can be either plain or paneled, which means that they have a blind embossed margin. (Blind embossing is like engraving, except there is no ink on the raised impression.) In years gone by, engravers inserted a sheet of tissue to insure that the engraving caused no smudges, but advanced engraving techniques have eliminated the need for it. If you wish to have tissue just for its look, stationers will provide sheets on request.

Once upon a time, convention decreed that there be two envelopes in a wedding invitation: an inner envelope holding the invitation (with the folded edge first) and enclosures (all facing the back flap); and an outer envelope into which the inner is inserted, unsealed, with the flap facing away from you. This is still correct—but nowadays, given concerns about conservation, it is equally correct to have one envelope.

You should order invitations three months before your wedding to allow time for engraving, addressing, stuffing, and mailing. Most engravers will accommodate a request to provide the envelopes before the invitations are done. This will allow you (or a calligrapher, if you choose) more time for addressing.

Ideally, wedding invitations should be mailed four to six weeks before the wedding. In the case of holiday weddings or summer weddings, you may wish to take the precaution of mailing your invitations eight weeks in advance. To make certain you are putting on the correct postage, have both the reply envelope with its enclosure and the complete invitation weighed at your local post office.

WORDING FOR FORMAL INVITATIONS

Some of the conventions of formal wedding invitations include requesting the "honour" (spelled with a "u") of a guest's presence for the invitation to the ceremony, while requesting the "pleasure" of a guest's company for the reception; spelling out the numbers in a date; referring to half hours as "half after"; writing out the title "Doctor"; using middle names in full, rather than initials; and not including an R.S.V.P. on an invitation to the ceremony alone. Wording on formal invitations allows for few variations.

For a church ceremony the wording is as follows:

Doctor and Mrs. Chandler Reeves Sinclair
request the honour of your presence
at the marriage of their daughter
Carson Blaine
to
Mr. Jared Christopher Rand
Saturday, the ninth of September
at half after four o'clock
St. James Episcopal Church
New York City

An alternative for a Roman Catholic ceremony might be:

Mr. and Mrs. Anthony Simon Perelli
request the honour of your presence
at the marriage of their daughter
Carla Louise
to
Mr. Michael Joseph Grasso
and your participation
in the offering of the Nuptial Mass
Saturday, the third of June
at twelve o'clock
Sacred Heart Church
New York City

Wording for a synagogue wedding follows the same general format:

Mr. and Mrs. Marc Aaron Kamen
request the honour of your presence
at the marriage of their daughter
Rachel Brynne
to
Mr. Peter Eric Dane
Saturday, the twentieth of June
at nine o'clock
Beekman Place Synagogue
New York City

A more traditionally Jewish invitation differs slightly:

Mr. and Mrs. Marc Aaron Kamen
Mr. and Mrs. Noah Samuel Dane
request the honour of your presence
at the marriage of
Rachel Brynne Kamen
and
Peter Eric Dane
(etc.)

It might also read:

Mr. and Mrs. Marc Aaron Kamen
request the honour of your presence
at the marriage of their daughter
Rachel Brynne
and
Mr. Peter Eric Dane
son of Mr. and Mrs. Noah Samuel Dane
(etc.)

Families or couples may choose to have their invitation printed in English and in Hebrew on facing pages.

When the guest list for the wedding ceremony and reception are the same, the invitation may be combined:

FRED MARCUS

Mr. and Mrs. Randall Avery Harmon
request the honour of your presence
at the marriage of their daughter
Abigail Louise
to
Mr. Bailey Devers Carver
Saturday, the fourteenth of September
at half after five o'clock
Church of the Heavenly Rest
New York City
and afterward at the reception
The Plaza
Black tie

Or:

Mr. and Mrs. Justin Carl Tannenbaum
request the pleasure of your company
at the marriage of their daughter
Perri Kate
to
Mr. Jeremy Reese Littell
Saturday, the twenty-first of November
at half after eight o'clock
The Plaza
New York City
Black tie

If more guests are invited to the wedding ceremony than to the reception, a separate card is enclosed with the invitation for guests being invited to the reception:

Reception
immediately following the ceremony
The Plaza
New York City
The favour of a reply is requested

When the wedding ceremony is private and most guests are being invited only to the reception, the invitation to the ceremony may be issued orally. The wording for the reception invitation is:

Mr. and Mrs. Theodore Elliot Keogh
request the pleasure of your company
at the wedding reception
of their daughter
Caitlin Bridget
and
Mr. Mario Ecco
Sunday, the fifth of May
at half after twelve o'clock
The Plaza
New York City

Invitations to the wedding ceremony alone do not include a request for a reply. Invitations to the ceremony and the reception—or to a reception alone—may say "R.S.V.P.," "R.s.v.p.," or "The favour of a reply is requested."

Special circumstances call for modifications to the standard wording.

If only one of the bride's parents is living, the invitation is issued in that parent's name alone:

Mr. Conor Reid Loughlin
requests the honour of your presence
at the marriage of his daughter
Kit Paine Loughlin
to
Mr. Brady Allen Lawrence

(etc.)

Mr. and Mrs. Steven Leber
request the honour of your presence
at the marriage of their daughter

Michelle Ann
to
Michael Paul
son of
Mr. and Mrs. Eugene Roberts
Saturday, the twentieth of March
Nineteen hundred and ninety-three
at half after seven o'clock
The Plaza Hotel
New York City

Black Tie

Professional titles—for doctors, dentists, veterinarians, members of the clergy, judges, and others—are always used in the case of the bridegroom or the father of the bride. (This is not generally true for men who hold academic degrees except in instances where they are always referred to as "Dr.")

Convention still decrees that the mother of the bride does not use her title, and that the bride does only if she is issuing the invitation with her groom:

The honour of your presence
is requested
at the marriage of
Dr. Natalie Sands
and
Mr. Nelson Robles

(etc.)

However, many people have come to feel strongly about this issue and choose to flout convention:

Dr. Alana and Mr. Thomas Barton
request the honour of your presence

(etc.)

Dr. Inez and Dr. Richard Morales
request the honour of your presence

(etc.)

Military titles are used when the groom, the father of the bride, or the bride is a member of the armed services or is on active duty in the reserves.

The same considerations that apply to professional titles for the mother of the bride would pertain if she is a member of the armed forces or on active duty with the reserves.

For grooms who are army officers with the rank of captain or higher, and for navy officers beginning with the rank of lieutenant, senior grade, this is the proper form:

Captain Derek Holmes
United States Army

Officers with lower ranks use the following form:

John Raymond
Ensign, United States Navy

For those in the army, "Lieutenant" is used regardless of whether it refers to a first or second lieutenant.

Reserve officers on active duty follow the same style, with one variation:

Colonel Jared Tynan
Army of the United States

For noncommissioned officers and enlisted men, including rank and branch of service on the invitation is a matter of personal choice. High-ranking officers continue to use both title and branch of service after retirement:

General Bryce Carillo
United States Army, retired

The father of the bride simply uses his title in the same way a professional might use his:

Major and Mrs. Michael Han

request the honour of your presence

(etc.)

A bride who is on active duty would use the following form:

Mr. and Mrs. Trevor Curtis Mallon

request the honour of your presence

at the marriage of their daughter

Lara Nicole

Lieutenant, United States Army

When a wedding is given by the bride's siblings or other relatives, the invitation is worded accordingly:

Mr. Peter Rothschild

requests the honour of your presence

at the marriage of his sister

Alexandra

(etc.)

If more than one sibling is giving the wedding, their names are listed in age order, from oldest to youngest:

Mr. Peter Rothschild
Mr. and Mrs. Eric Zachary Jordan
Miss Julianna Rothschild

request the honour of your presence

at the marriage of their sister

Alexandra

(etc.)

For other relatives:

Doctor and Mrs. Simon Theodore Byrne

request the honour of your presence

at the marriage of their niece

Bridget Katharine Shane

(etc.)

A double wedding for two sisters lists the elder's name first:

Mr. and Mrs. Gabriel Sontag

request the honour of your presence

at the marriage of their daughters

Hallie Justine

to

Mr. Evan Blake Shahn

and

Kyla Paige

to

Mr. Luke Samuel Trask

(etc.)

In the case of a second marriage, a young widow's parents may issue invitations as they did for the first marriage; however, they should use her married name:

Mr. and Mrs. Paul Stanley Latham
request the honour of your presence
at the marriage of their daughter
Karen Latham Thompson

(etc.)

A divorcée's invitation may follow the same form with whatever name she is actually using: either her maiden name and former husband's name or her middle and maiden names. If a widow or divorcée no longer has parents who are living, or if she is no longer a very young woman, she would more properly send out her own invitations:

The honour of your presence
is requested
at the marriage of
Mrs. Richard Arnold Pastor
and
Mr. Timothy Curran Case

(etc.)

A divorcée may use her title or choose to drop it:

The honour of your presence
is requested
at the marriage of
Mrs. Amy Lindt Sanders

(etc.)

Or:

The honour of your presence
is requested at the marriage of
Amy Lindt Sanders

(etc.)

There are circumstances under which the groom's parents may elect to give the wedding—if the bride's family is too far away or unable to, if the bride's family refuses to accept the marriage, or if the bride has no family.

In such an event, the groom's family issues the invitations:

Mr. and Mrs. Nathaniel Jason Brandeis
request the honour of your presence
at the marriage of
Dr. Mayumi Hirata
to their son
Dr. Jeremy Royce Brandeis

(etc.)

The announcements are still sent by the bride's family. In the event that is not possible, the announcements may be sent by the groom's family and should include the names of the bride's parents.

If the bride's and groom's parents are giving the wedding jointly, the wording for a formal invitation is:

Mr. and Mrs. André Tyner
and
Dr. and Mrs. Grafton Warner
request the pleasure of your company
at the wedding reception of
Kyla Brett Tyner
and
Grafton Warner, Junior
(etc.)

WORDING FOR NONTRADITIONAL INVITATIONS

One advantage of a nontraditional invitation is that using your own words and referring to yourself in the first person may convey a greater feeling of warmth and genuineness than the standard formal invitation. Another advantage is that it offers more scope for creative design and use of color, an obvious choice being a color that reflects the general wedding color scheme.

In a nontraditional invitation, the ideal is to strike a balance that allows you to communicate something of your feelings without sounding mawkish or artificial. The simpler and more direct the language, the more impact it will have. Once again, it is important to remember that the purpose of the invitation is to convey information in a clear and gracious manner.

If you intend to compose your own wedding invitation, it may help to organize your thoughts if you break down the standard invitation into its component parts:

The names of the hostess and host
The nature of the event (wedding ceremony, reception, or both)
The bride's name
The groom's name
The time and place for the ceremony
The time and place for the reception
The request for a reply

This is the basic information that should be included—how you elect to frame the information is what personalizes it. For example, this might be sent from the parents of the bride:

Please share in our joy
as we celebrate the marriage of our daughter
Mackenzie Blaine
to
Tyrone Burton
on Saturday, the seventeenth of June
at seven o'clock
The Plaza
New York City
Cory and Michael Romney
R.S.V.P.

Something along these lines would be appropriate for an invitation being sent by both sets of parents:

We invite you to celebrate with us
at a wedding reception for
Aysha and Charles
Sunday, May fifteenth
at one o'clock
The Plaza
New York City
Keiva and Jamal Carr
Sondra and Raymond Nelson
Please send your reply to Keiva and Jamal
45 Ryman Place
New York City

Or, from a couple sending out their own invitation:

Please make our joyous occasion complete
Join us as we exchange our vows
and help us celebrate
the beginning of our new life together
Saturday, December third
at seven o'clock
The Plaza
New York City
Tara Cole and Chase Marin

R.S.V.P.
Tara Cole
19 Gracie Mews
New York City 10021

ADDRESSING THE INVITATIONS

Wedding envelopes are always addressed by hand. No abbreviations—except for "Mr." and "Mrs."—are used. If a middle name is used, it should be written out in full, as should all components of the address.

Both members of a married couple, and both members of an unmarried couple, should be addressed on the front of the envelope:

Mr. and Mrs. Vincent Scalfa

Mr. Conrad Parrish and Ms. Annika Reimer

When children are invited, the dictates of convention may conflict with circumstance or modern sensibility: If the invitation to a couple is meant to include their young daughter or daughters, their names may be written on the envelope below the parents' names:

Mr. and Mrs. Joel Baird
Miss Zoe Baird

Or:

Mr. and Mrs. Joel Baird
The Misses Baird

Boys, however, are supposed to receive their own invitations. Of course, one can bypass the question of unequal treatment simply by sending separate invitations to everyone. In any event, younger children may be sent joint invitations:

The Messrs. Randolph

Or, if there are brothers and sisters:

The Messrs. Randolph
The Misses Randolph

Children over thirteen should properly be sent separate invitations. And while it is still considered in poor taste to address an invitation to "Mr. and Mrs. Jared Randolph and Family," the complexity of some of today's combined households may preclude any other approach. An invitation addressed in such a way, however, is read to mean that *all* family members living at that address are being invited.

To indicate to a single friend or relative that they may invite a guest to accompany them, you may either enclose a note saying so or write "Mr. Daniel Marlon and guest" on the inner envelope (if you are using one) or on the outer envelope.

If you are using an inner envelope, the names that will appear on the mailing envelope should be written on it, in the following forms. For close relatives:

Aunt Claudia and Uncle Simon

For a married couple:

Mr. and Mrs. Wyeth

For a married couple with a young daughter:

Mr. and Mrs. Wyeth
Miss Elisa Wyeth

For several young children:

Lucas, Hannah, and Naomi

Another edict that should go by the wayside for practical considerations is the rule against putting return addresses on wedding invitations. Having the return address embossed or engraved on the envelope complies with postal requirements and is helpful to the recipient.

If additional cards—reception cards, transportation cards, and so forth are being included with the invitation, they should be placed in the inner envelope, if you are using one. If not, they may be placed in the outer envelope. The cards should face the flap and either be within the fold of a folded invitation or in front of an invitation with no fold, facing the person inserting them.

RESPONSE CARDS AND ENVELOPES

Etiquette experts may deplore the need for enclosing response cards with wedding invitations—good manners should dictate a prompt response to any invitation received—but most concede that they serve a practical purpose. Moreover, in many circles they represent the custom and are both expected and accepted.

Response cards are engraved in the same style as the invitation and are usually accompanied by a stamped, self-addressed envelope. They are the smallest card size the postal service accepts for mailing.

Floral Decoration

FLOWERS AND DECOR

There is probably no aspect of weddings that has changed so much over the years as what one used to think of simply as "flowers." Under that heading were included altar flowers, flowers to decorate the pews, a bridal bouquet (or two, if the bride wished to toss a substitute), attendants' bouquets, corsages, boutonnieres, a basket of posies for the flower girl, and centerpieces for the reception. Flowers were always an integral component of weddings, and to get them one sought out a florist.

Nowadays it is not merely a matter of arranging for the flowers but of establishing the overall "decor" of the wedding. The categories above remain, with new elements added: draperies, linens, special chairs, special coverings for chairs, lighting effects, topiaries, trees, trellises, candelabra, carpets, crystal, and any number of actual stage props—all integrated to transform a space and create the ambience desired. Or, one may wish to enhance an atmosphere that already exists—or to better showcase a space that needs little enhancement.

It should come as no surprise, then, that what was once the province of a "florist" is now the specialty of a "floral designer"—and, often, a highly skilled crew as well.

Flowers remain the focal point for the designer, but the ultimate goal is to coordinate *all* the visual aspects of your ceremony and celebration to blend harmoniously and set the tone you want.

Opposite: FROM THE WEDDING OF JANEY LIEBERMAN AND NEIL VOGEL. *Right Top:* THE RAW MATERIALS: CHAMPAGNE AND WHITE FRENCH TULIPS, ROSES, AND ORCHIDS. FROM THE WEDDING OF ALLISON LAMBERT AND HOWARD LUTNICK.

PERRI PELTZ AND ERIC RUTTENBERG'S BRIDAL TABLE. COVERED WITH
AN ANTIQUE CLOTH FROM THE BRIDE'S GRANDMOTHER, THE CENTERPIECES
INCORPORATED FAMILY HEIRLOOMS FILLED WITH AN ARRAY OF WHITE
GARDEN ROSES ACCENTED BY VIBRANTLY COLORED BERRIES, APRICOTS,
BLACK GRAPES, AND IVY.

The options are limitless—from minimalist to opulent to fantastical—so you should
begin with whatever mental picture you have of your dream wedding. What is the mood or
overall style you see? A kind of rustic, woodsy simplicity? The sun-dappled look of a meadow?
An English country garden? The stylized glamour of a 1930s ocean liner or an Art Deco night-
club? Something Victorian? Something spare and coolly elegant, something tropically lush and
exotic, or something candlelit and romantic, out of a fairy tale?

(In the absence of any clear mental image or confirmed preference, start poring over
magazines and books and looking at old films to see what appeals to you. Or, begin with what

you know you *don't* want. It's a perfectly valid way to start. In any event, each designer will have books of his or her own to show you and you can get ideas from them.)

Whatever your inclination, a skilled floral designer can translate what is in your mind's eye into the decor for your wedding. But to do that, the designer must know something of what you have in mind.

Other considerations are more prosaic. Where is the wedding to be held? What does the space look like? What will you and your attendants be wearing? What time of year and what time of day have you chosen? And, of course, what is your budget?

The top floral designers agree that most clients come as referrals from former clients, either directly or because they have attended a

FROM THE WEDDING OF
NICOLE MITCHELL AND
EDDIE MURPHY.

FRED MARCUS

Pages 68 and 69:
FROM THE WEDDING OF
ALEXANDRA GARCIA AND
STEVEN COHEN.
PHOTO BY FRED MARCUS

Left: FROM THE WEDDING OF
JILL SCHWARTZBERG AND
DENNIS SHIELDS.

wedding and admired the decor. If you have been to a wedding that *looked* beautiful, you might call the bride to ask whether she would recommend her designer. (One clear advantage of this sort of personal recommendation is that, apart from the question of talent, you may get some sense of whether the designer is professional, responsive, and reliable.) Your wedding consultant, if you have hired one, will certainly know the most creative and reliable designers in your area. Other wedding professionals and suppliers are likely sources, as are bridal magazines.

What are you actually getting when you hire a floral designer? At best, you are engaging the creativity and expertise of a professional—someone capable of designing, acquiring, producing, and carrying out all the decorations for your ceremony and reception, as well as the flowers you and your bridal party will wear and carry.

There are several ways to work with a designer. One is to give the designer whatever information you have—including your preferences, your special needs, and your budget—and allow her or him to create something original for you. (This approach, as any designer will tell you, is a designer's idea of heaven.) It is unquestionably the best way to elicit what a designer does best. For an artist—and make no mistake, that is what a designer is—nothing rivals the opportunity to create something fresh and original. Once the proposed designs are presented to you, you and the designer can collaborate to alter or eliminate elements you don't like.

Alternately, you can come to a designer with very specific requests—if you will, with a design of your own—and ask the designer to execute it for you. If you plan to use this approach, you would do well to rely on the judgment, experience, and expertise of whomever you engage. No matter how glorious your idea, it is nothing but a pipe dream if it can't be executed well, or within your budget.

Another possibility is to request that the designer re-create something he or she did for another event. While no one minds the implied compliment—after all, you admired a design scheme well enough to want it for yourself—every event is slightly different, and you should allow the designer to suggest customized modifications that will serve you better.

Or your approach can be somewhere in between.

For the sake of clear communication, prepare for your first meeting by collecting tear sheets from magazines, photo spreads from books, sketches or descriptions of dress styles of the wedding party, and swatches of material from your gown, the attendants' dresses, and, if possible, your mother's and the groom's mother's dresses. A list of flowers that have some special meaning for you and your fiancé, or are personal favorites—not to mention any flowers you can't abide—is also helpful. Bear in mind that flowers are not merely used for effect, they have

symbolic meaning as well. You might even consult a book on the language of *Above:* DAIS TABLE
flowers when you are considering your selection.

If you have your heart set on out-of-season, special varieties that can be gotten only from
hothouses or that need to be imported, be prepared to pay dearly—particularly if you envision
a floral scheme that calls for masses of blooms. Seasonal flowers, locally grown, are always the
best choice if your budget is limited. A designer can usually help you find acceptable compro-
mises between your heart's desire and the means at your disposal.

THE BRIDAL BOUQUET

The shape and composition of a bridal bouquet is best determined by such considerations as the
formality of the wedding gown, its style and fabric, and the bride's height—as well as personal
preferences and the overall color scheme.

Fred Marcus

Left: MARJORIE ESTEROW LEVINE.

Below: ELISA CRESCI McEVOY.

Fred Marcus

Bridal bouquets are generally fashioned in three basic styles: the *cascade bouquet,* in which a cluster of blooms spills gently to a triangular point; the *crescent,* or *arm bouquet,* which nestles in the crook of the arm and drapes down; and the classic *nosegay,* a small, tightly gathered circle of flowers. If your dress calls for less formal arrangements, a sheaf of long-stemmed blooms or a loosely gathered, hand-tied bouquet of wildflowers could look lovely. Sometimes even a single long-stemmed flower can create a really striking effect.

If you are torn between wanting to toss your bouquet and preserving it as a keepsake, the designer can create a simpler version for you to toss.

SARAH MERIANS

SARAH MERIANS

Above: FROM THE WEDDING OF
ELIZABETH SCHWARTZ AND KEN FISHER.

Left: DENNIS AND JILL SHIELDS.

ATTENDANTS' BOUQUETS, CORSAGES, FLORAL HEADPIECES, FLOWER GIRL'S BASKET, AND BOUTONNIERES

Above: BOUQUETS BY OPPIZI & CO.

Left: FROM THE WEDDING OF MICHELLE LEBER AND MICHAEL ROBERTS.

Below: CARLA STRANIERO BARONE AND HER ATTENDANTS.

FRED MARCUS

FRED MARCUS

FLOWERS FOR THE CEREMONY

Left: FROM THE WEDDING OF
ELISA CRESCI AND
TIM McEVOY.
Below: ELISA CRESCI COMING
DOWN THE AISLE OF THE
CHURCH OF THE HOLY
TRINITY ON THE ARM OF HER
FATHER LAURENCE.

FRED MARCUS

FRED MARCUS

Above: NICOLE AND EDDIE MURPHY'S DAIS TABLE

FRED MARCUS

DENIS GARTNER

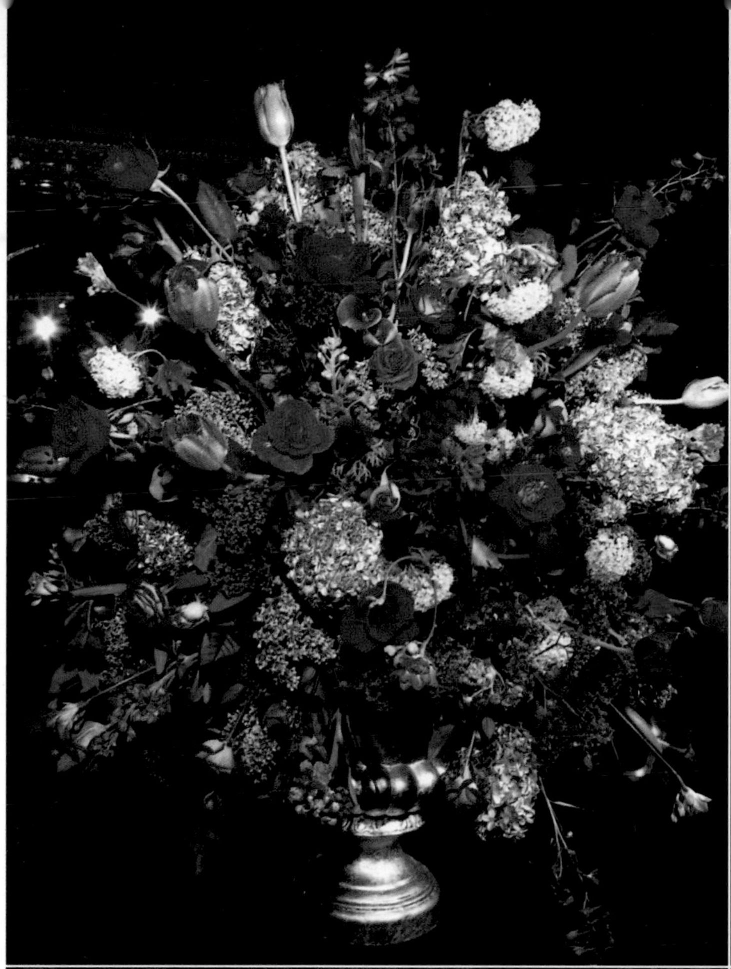

Fred Marcus

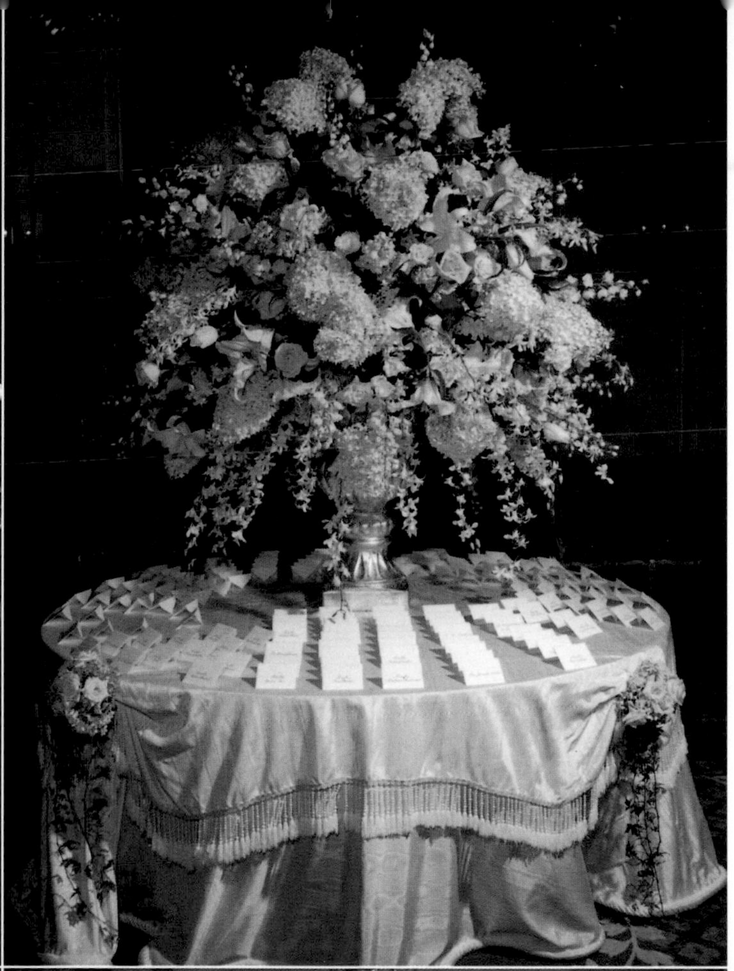

Fred Marcus

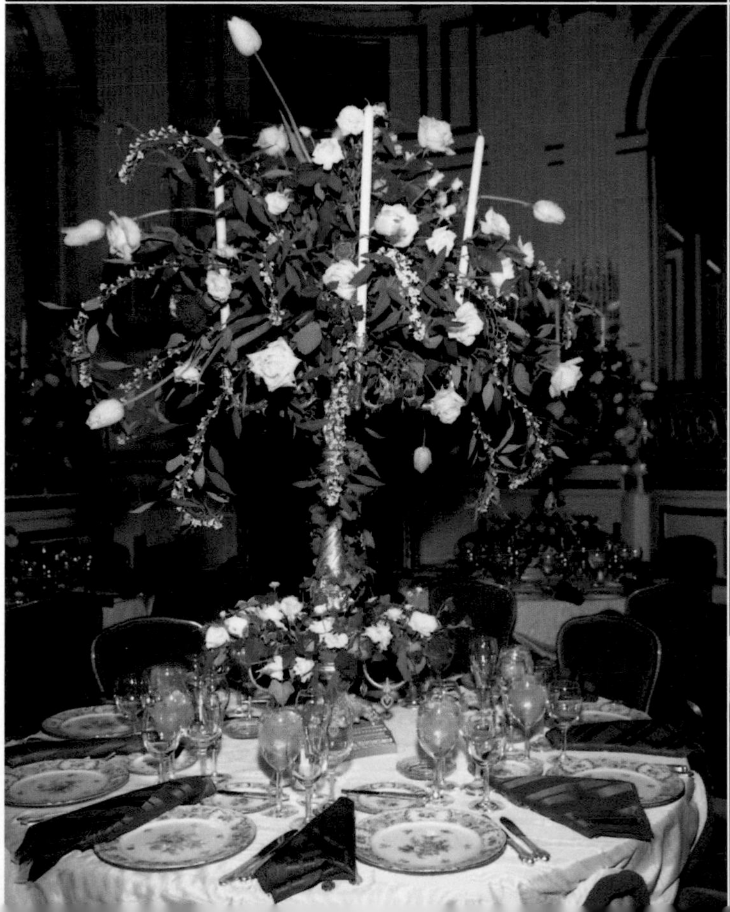

Fred Marcus

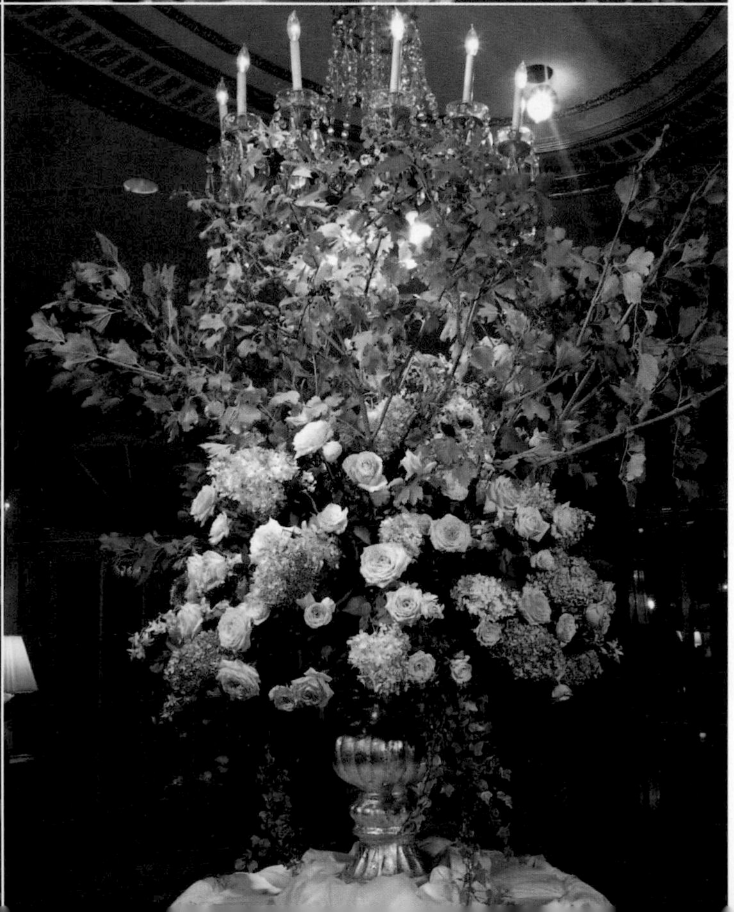

Fred Marcus

Music

P oll the top wedding consultants in New York on what single element can make or break a wedding reception and the response is unanimous: the music.

Music provides a continuous thread that, woven through the celebration, establishes the ambience, signals and underscores changes in emotional tempo, stirs memories, reinforces custom and tradition, and brings people to their feet. Having music at a Jewish wedding is considered a religious obligation, going all the way back to an ancient custom of playing a flute before the bride and groom. Music allows you and your guests to express ardor, enthusiasm, communal identity, and collective joy—and helps create memories that linger for years to come.

It begins with the ceremony.

FRED MARCUS

Left: FROM THE WEDDING OF DEBORAH GALANT AND PAUL LAZAR.

Opposite Page, Top Left: FROM THE WEDDING OF MARLA MAPLES AND DONALD TRUMP; *Top Right:* THE PLAZA'S OWN PALM COURT MUSICIANS SETTING UP; *Bottom:* GYPSY VIOLINS SERENADED GUESTS DURING PERRI PELTZ AND ERIC RUTTENBERG'S WEDDING DINNER WITH SOFT, ROMANTIC MUSIC.

Below: CARLA STRANIERO BARONE
DANCES WITH HER FATHER,
DR. CHARLES STRANIERO. THIRTY
YEARS EARLIER, THE PLAZA'S GRAND
BALLROOM WAS THE SITE OF THE
STRANIEROS' OWN WEDDING.

There are essentially four segments of the ceremony that call for music: the period when guests are being seated, the processional, the recessional, and the period during which the guests are leaving. For the most part, ceremonies are conducted without music, although couples may choose to incorporate musical elements.

For a church or temple service, questions of what music may be played when and by whom must be taken up with the minister, priest, or rabbi. The church or temple will most likely have an organ and possibly a choir and soloist. You may be permitted to supplement this with hired musicians or taped music. Your musical selections should be discussed with the organist or choirmaster. Ironically, you may find the two melodies most associated with weddings—Wagner's "Bridal Chorus" from *Lohengrin* ("Here Comes the Bride") and Mendelssohn's "Wedding March" from *A Midsummer Night's Dream*—rejected as inappropriate. (Some churches consider them too secular and prefer more religious hymns or marches, while some rabbis feel that because of the composers' well-known personal beliefs, their compositions have no place in Jewish weddings.)

MUSIC AT NANCY SAMPSON AND JOSHUA COHEN'S WEDDING FEATURED THE BEACH BOYS.

If you are bringing in outside musicians or are using taped music, you should schedule a meeting between the group's leader, or whoever will be in charge of the tape, and the organist or choirmaster so that everything can be coordinated properly.

Music before the processional should serve to welcome incoming guests and put them in a serene and anticipatory mood for the ceremony. The music need not be particularly solemn, so long as it is not inappropriately frivolous.

The processional calls for a majestic and beautiful melody that sets the tempo for a slow, stately walk down the aisle. The recessional is ringing and joyous; it signals: Let the celebration begin!

Music at the reception offers a much wider range of possibilities. If there is a cocktail hour, the best choices are lively songs and melodies from the jazz, swing, and Broadway show tune repertoire or popular classical selections. Guests should be aware of the music but able to speak comfortably to one another.

Unless all of your guests come from the same background and belong to a similar age group, an orchestra or band with a reasonably wide repertoire—1930s and 1940s Big Band tunes, swing, Dixieland, Latin, rock, salsa—is your wisest choice. As hosts, you want *all* your guests to dance, and that means providing music to which many different people can dance.

The music should be loud enough to beckon your guests onto the dance floor but not so loud that they can't converse. Too-loud music is often a grievance at weddings.

HIRING MUSICIANS

The number of musicians you hire is usually determined by the following considerations:

The size of your budget.
How many segments of the wedding you wish to cover and how many hours that entails.
Space and acoustics.
The complexity of your arrangements. (Is each segment to be covered in a different location, requiring the musicians to set up several times?)

Whether or not you want continuous music.
Whether or not you want continuous dancing.
Whether you plan to have a DJ and a postdinner disco.
Whether the band can and will provide its own formal attire.

The best ways to find musicians, if you haven't heard a band or a group you like, is to ask for recommendations from friends. Most bands provide tapes that give you an idea of the range of their sound. Set up appointments with the band leaders or agency representatives of the outfits you are considering and try to provide them with as much information as you can about what you want. If you are dealing with a reputable, professional orchestra or production organization, you should be able to rely on their advice, particularly when budget constraints necessitate some concessions. No one is better placed than a professional to show you how to scale back without compromising quality.

Some things to establish when hiring musicians:

Basic charges.
Overtime—Is the band available for overtime? (You don't want your musicians packing up to go somewhere else with your party in full swing.) What are the rates for overtime?
Breaks (number of breaks, how long, who will fill in).
Attire.

Schedule of events (for example, bridal couple's first entrance, toasts, *motzi* blessing over challah, first dance, bride's dance with her father, groom's dance with his mother, cake cutting, special ethnic dances, and so on).
Special requests.
Backup policy (in the event that a musician becomes ill).

Whether you hire a production organization, a single band, or individual instrumentalists and soloists, you should have a formal contract with each covering all the items listed above.

Photography and Video

Apart from your memories, your wedding photographs are the most tangible mementos of the day you were married. They should be worthy of the occasion. Wedding pictures not only offer a lifetime of pleasure and recollection to their participants, they become heirlooms handed down to coming generations.

Once again, personal recommendations are the soundest way to begin looking for a photographer. When you have compiled a list, make appointments to see each. Remember that top photographers—and top wedding photographers, especially—are in very great demand and tend to be booked far in advance.

MICHELLE LEBER ROBERTS

Look carefully at the work you are shown. Style and quality count in equal measure: You want well-taken, well-lit photos that are flattering to you and your guests, capture the spirit of your wedding, and cover all of the special events. The photos should be beautifully printed and handsomely bound.

Your rapport with the photographer and his or her assistants is also critical. Really fine photography demands a sense of confidence in the person behind the camera. You want to feel relaxed and unself-conscious, particularly in the posed photos. You don't want to entrust such a task to anyone you find intrusive or indifferent—it will show up in the results.

Right: MARLA AND DONALD TRUMP *Below Left:* ERIC AND LISA BLUMENCRANZ. *Below Right:* ALLISON AND HOWARD LUTNICK.

FRED MARCUS

DENIS GARTNER

DENIS REGGIE

Bear in mind the following considerations when you are engaging the photographer:

The size of your budget.

How many aspects of the preparations and the wedding you wish to cover, how many people that will logistically require, and how many hours that will entail.

The complexity of your arrangements. (Is each segment to be covered in a different location, requiring the photographer to travel? What are the limitations that may be imposed and the special lighting needs?)

The style of photography you are seeking. (Don't be shy about bringing along photo books or tear sheets to illustrate the look you are after. If what you want is technically impossible given your budget—or impossible to reproduce at an event like a wedding—it's up to the professional to either convince you of this or gracefully decline the job.)

Ratio of candid shots to posed groups and portraits.

Settle questions of appropriate attire. Ask whether the photographer and crew can provide their own formal attire.

Basic charges and precisely what this covers.

Extras. Can the photographer and crew stay as long as you need them? What are the charges for extra proofs, additional albums, additional album pages?

Schedule of events (for example, bridal couple's first entrance, toasts, *motzi* blessing over challah, first dance, bride's dance with her father, groom's dance with his mother, cake cutting, special ethnic dances, and so forth).

Special requests.

Backup policy (in the event that the photographer or an assistant becomes ill).

How long till you see proofs?

How soon after your selections are made can you expect your albums?

You should have a formal contract covering all the items listed above.

Video demands much the same process. When you view the videographer's samples be sensitive to the flow of the action; sharp, well-focused, nonjerky images; smooth editing; and an allover professional look. Be sure to establish what you want covered and how it is to be done: Video lights are very bright, and having a camera bear down on you or your guests can be extremely intrusive to anyone not accustomed to it. Good video demands far more compromise than still photography because it is essentially all documentary—there are no retakes.

Bridal Registry and Gifts

For those who would argue that bridal registries are useful only to couples who have the money to buy everything they *really* need, take heart: Alongside gravy boats and fish slices you can now add his-and-her duffel bags or aerobics equipment. The list of items for which you can register has grown considerably, and you would be surprised at some of the stores that offer this service.

You should make your selections before you send out your invitations. Be sure to select individual items in a reasonably wide price range.

FRED MARCUS

The Wedding Ceremony

The essence of a marriage ceremony is that it exists to sanctify and legalize the union of a man and a woman into a lifelong partnership. Whether the arrangements are simple or elaborate, traditional or a blend of traditions and more personalized elements, the wedding ceremony is one of the most meaningful and moving rituals of life. It should be approached with a sense of care, thoughtfulness, and dignity to ensure that it remains one of life's most memorable rituals for the bride and groom.

FROM THE WEDDING OF ALLISON LAMBERT AND HOWARD LUTNICK.

PROTOCOL FOR A PROTESTANT CEREMONY

Family members and honored guests should be seated within the ribbon or in reserved pews at the front. When the groom's parents arrive, the groom's mother is escorted to her seat, followed by her husband.

Five minutes before the ceremony, the bride's mother should be escorted to her seat in the front row. After the aisle runner is rolled down the aisle, the bride's father takes his place with the bride and attendants take their places in the proper order for the processional.

The minister, groom, and best man enter the church, the groom and best man taking their places to the right of the aisle, facing the congregation.

THE PROCESSIONAL: The processional is led off by pairs of ushers walking in a slow and measured pace down the aisle. Junior

Below: FROM THE WEDDING OF SUSAN HARVEY AND DARIN RAMEY.

FRED MARCUS

ushers, if there are any, go next, followed by junior bridesmaids. Bridesmaids follow in double or single file, depending on their number. Next comes the maid or matron of honor (if there are both, the maid of honor precedes the matron of honor). The flower girl proceeds, followed by the ring bearer. To achieve the full visual effect of a processional, even spaces should be maintained between each couple or person, as should a slow, even, stately pace.

The bride enters, on the right arm of her father. They walk down the aisle to the altar, where the groom waits, flanked by his best man.

Where the attendants stand when they reach the front of the church varies, depending on what works best. Once the bride arrives at her groom's side she takes her arm from her father and transfers her flowers to her left arm. The groom takes her right arm and places it through his left, with her hand resting at his elbow. If they prefer, they may choose to stand side by side, or they may hold hands.

The bride's father remains until he is asked by the minister, "Who gives this woman to be married?" He may either reply, "I do," or, as is increasingly the case, "Her mother and I do."

In the absence of her father, the bride may choose to be escorted by a male relative or family friend. The question "Who gives this woman to be married?" is then answered by the bride's mother from her pew.

Some brides, flouting tradition, elect to have their mother accompany them down the aisle, or a bride may walk down the aisle unescorted.

When the pastor turns to walk to the altar, the bride and groom follow, as do the maid of honor, best man, flower girl, and ring bearer. The bride hands her bouquet to the maid of honor. When the ring is needed, the best man takes it from the ring bearer's cushion—or produces it himself—and hands it to the minister. In a double-ring ceremony, the maid of honor then hands the groom's ring to the minister. (The bride must remember to transfer her engagement ring to her right hand before the ceremony since the wedding band should not be put on outside the engagement ring.)

Once the ceremony is over and the bride and groom have kissed, the recessional music begins. The maid of honor returns the bride's bouquet and straightens her train. The order of the recessional is bride and groom, flower girl and ring bearer, maid of honor and best man. Each usher pairs off with a bridesmaid and they proceed down the aisle together. If the numbers are uneven, attendants may repeat the processional order or the extra ushers may walk in pairs at the end. A lone usher should be the last in the recessional.

PROTOCOL FOR A ROMAN CATHOLIC CEREMONY

Roman Catholic marriages are traditionally preceded by the publishing of banns (either from the pulpit or in the church calendar) three times before the wedding. The ceremony itself is often centered around a nuptial mass.

Most details are the same as those for a Protestant ceremony with some exceptions: The father of the bride escorts his daughter down the aisle but does not give her away; he returns to the front pew as soon as she has given her hand to the groom. The placement of the bridal party varies from church to church, and may depend on whether or not a nuptial mass follows the wedding ceremony.

Opposite: ELISA AND LAURENCE CRESCI.

Left: DR. ROBERT BARONE AND CARLA STRANIERO

FRED MARCUS

PROTOCOL FOR A JEWISH CEREMONY

Jewish tradition calls for a bride and groom to be regarded as royalty, complete with accompanying royal entourage. (Serving the wedding king and queen is both an honor and an obligation.) The variations in processional order are as numerous as the degree of orthodoxy, the incorporation of practices from all over the Diaspora, or the ideological inclinations of the bridal couple could allow.

Bearing this in mind, the following is a generally acceptable order for an American Jewish wedding processional: The ushers lead off, followed by the bridesmaids. Next follow the rabbi—with the cantor, if there is one—and the best man. The groom then walks down the aisle, accompanied by both his parents. The maid of honor follows, then the bride, escorted by both

Left & Above:
FROM THE WEDDING OF
MICHELLE LEBER AND
MICHAEL ROBERTS.

FRED MARCUS

FRED MARCUS

parents. (Orthodox and traditional Jewish brides are always veiled as a symbol of modesty and to commemorate Rebecca, who, as Genesis tells us, "took the veil and covered herself" when she first saw her husband-to-be.)

The bride and groom proceed to the *chuppah,* a bridal canopy, open on all sides, that is invested with centuries of symbolism: as a reminder of the tents of nomadic ancestors (particularly Abraham, of legendary hospitality, whose tent was open on all sides so visitors would always be assured of their welcome); as a consummation of the betrothal; and as a symbol of the new home to be shared. Custom differs as to who should rightfully stand under the *chuppah* with the bridal couple, ranging from the bride and groom alone, to honor attendants, to as many family members as fit, to guests who participate in the ceremony. The question is most properly addressed to the officiating rabbi.

Once again, ceremonies may vary greatly, but most generally they comprise a greeting and an invocation; a blessing for the first cup of wine; a sip of wine by the groom and then the bride; the groom's giving and the bride's acceptance of the ring; the reading of the *ketubah* (the marriage contract) by the rabbi—who then hands it to the groom to give to his bride; an address by the rabbi to the congregation and the couple; the Seven Blessings; a sip from the second cup of wine; and the pronouncement of marriage by the rabbi. The ceremony concludes with what is arguably the best known custom of Jewish weddings: the breaking of a wineglass by the groom.

The recessional is led off by the bridal couple, followed by both sets of parents, the maid of honor and best man, the rabbi and cantor, and the bridesmaids and ushers.

The Receiving Line

For many, the thought of a receiving line is an ordeal. Greeting and receiving the good wishes of a great many people—some barely known—call for a great deal of aplomb. Nevertheless, the receiving line serves an important function, especially at a large wedding, as it allows the bride and groom to meet all the guests and ensures that guests can be certain of meeting each member of the bridal couple as well as their parents.

The bride and groom may have their receiving line immediately after the ceremony or they may wait until the posed photos are taken and form the line at the site of the reception.

The mother of the bride stands first in line to greet the guests. Fathers are not

A RADIANT ELISA CRESCI
MCEVOY AND TIM MCEVOY
GREET GUESTS ON THE
RECEIVING LINE.

FRED MARCUS

FRED MARCUS

required to stand in the receiving line—they may feel more useful circulating among the guests. If the bride's father chooses to take his place in the line, it is next to his wife. The groom's mother follows, with her husband directly after her. (If the bride's father is in the receiving line, the groom's father should be as well.)

To avoid any embarrassment to themselves, or confusion to the guests, divorced parents generally do not stand in the line together. The custodial parent and stepparent, or the parents who are giving the wedding, should be in the line. If, however, there is no awkwardness to militate against it, both couples may stand in the line, but they should be separated by the groom's parents.

The bride stands next to her mother-in-law, with the groom alongside her. Bridesmaids stand in the receiving line only at the bride's pleasure. (It should be remembered that an overlong receiving line can be taxing on participants and guests alike.) As a rule, young children do not stand in the line.

A graceful way to keep things moving smoothly is for each person in the receiving line to introduce the guest to the next in line before turning to greet the next guest.

In Jewish ceremonies where the bridal couple observe the traditional *yichud* (a brief ceremonial seclusion where they break the day-long fast customary for brides and grooms), the receiving line is often abandoned.

FRED MARCUS

MAYOR DAVID DINKINS, DONALD TRUMP, AND MARLA MAPLES TRUMP

The Reception

There are many ways to celebrate a wedding. It is neither the choice of one style over another nor the lavishness of the hospitality that signals to guests your wish that they share in your happiness—it is the genuineness of that wish that will make the event truly unforgettable.

If you choose the best of what you like and can afford—and maintain sufficient control to see that everything is executed as well as can be—you can't miss.

WEDDING CAKES

Wedding cakes have come a long way since the barley cake the Romans made as an offering to Jupiter. (Today's ritual of bride and groom feeding one another a bit of cake is another improvement over days of yore: After tasting their cake, Roman bridegrooms crumbled the rest over the bride's head to bless her with fertility.)

The barley cake eventually became a stack of sweetened buns—or small, spiced currant cakes, depending on where you were—but it was the addition of icing that set the stage for the splendor of the modern-day wedding cake.

Preceding Page, Clockwise, from Top Left
FROM THE WEDDING OF ALEXANDRA GARCIA AND
STEVEN COHEN (FRED MARCUS), FROM THE WEDDING OF NANCY SAMPSON AND
JOSHUA COHEN (FRED MARCUS), MICHELLE LEBER ROBERTS WITH HER
FATHER, STEVE (FRED MARCUS), FROM THE WEDDING OF LISA FEINBERG
AND ERIC BLUMENCRANZ (DENIS GARTNER), FROM THE WEDDING OF
MICHELLE LEBER AND MICHAEL ROBERTS (FRED MARCUS),
FROM THE WEDDING OF NANCY SAMPSON AND JOSHUA COHEN (FRED MARCUS),
SUSAN HARVEY RAMEY WITH HER FATHER,
AUTHOR LAWRENCE HARVEY (FRED MARCUS), FROM THE WEDDING OF
NICOLE SILVER AND BRAD SCHEFLER (FRED MARCUS), *Center:* FROM THE
WEDDING OF ALEXANDRA GARCIA AND STEVEN COHEN (FRED MARCUS).

Right: SYLVIA WEINSTOCK AND HER HUSBAND, BEN, ASSEMBLING
DONALD AND MARLA TRUMP'S NINE-TIER WEDDING CAKE.

Left: PLAZA PARISIEN
CAKE.

Below: PASTRY CHEF
ERIC GOUTEYRON
APPLYING THE
FINISHING TOUCHES.

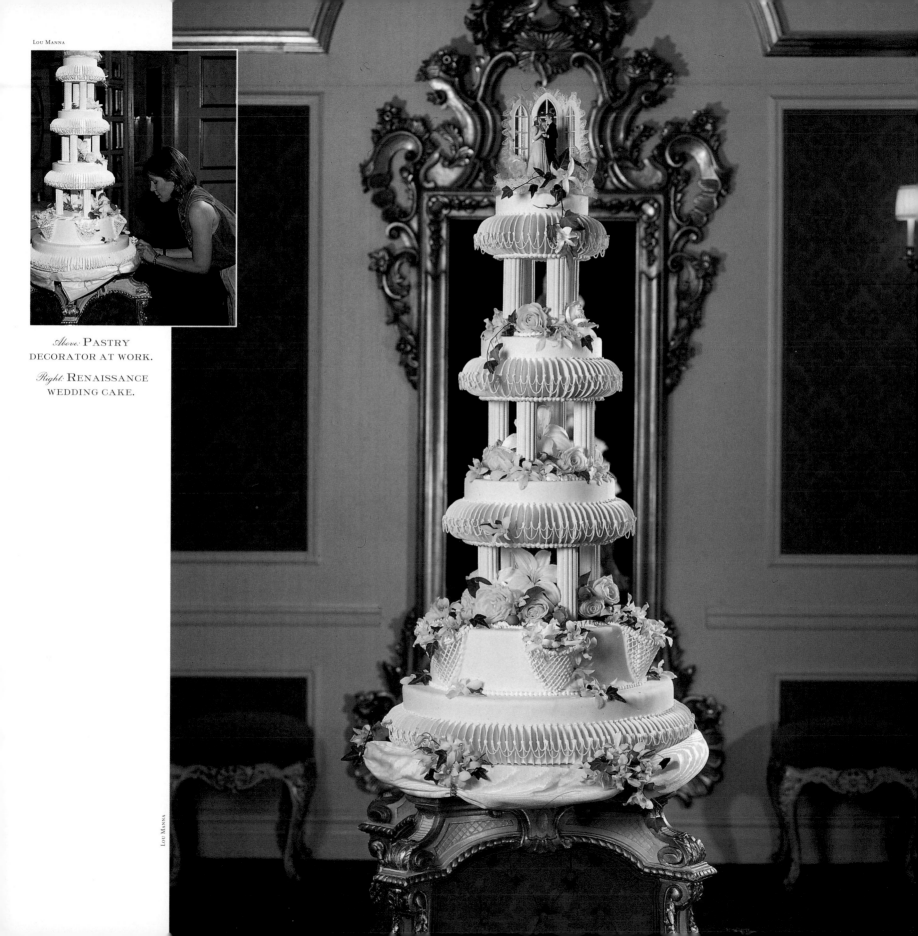

Above: PASTRY
DECORATOR AT WORK.

Right: RENAISSANCE
WEDDING CAKE.

The wedding cake, whether it is a sculpted wonder of delicate design or a many-tiered, garlanded, architectural triumph, is as symbolic of nuptials as the bride's white gown and veil or the bouquet she tosses. The artisans of the wedding cake are surely the royalty of the baking world. Their creations are probably the most painstaking and labor-intensive aspect of the wedding.

These are some of our favorites, including creations by Sylvia Weinstock, cake baker supreme, and the Plaza's own premiere pastry chef.

Above: GROOM'S CAKE.

Right: WEDDING CAKE AS A BEAUTIFUL BASKET.

Opposite: LES CASCADES WEDDING CAKE.

LOU MANNA

Wedding Menus

*T*hink of wedding food and you think of a *feast.* Whether you are planning an elegant brunch, a more elaborate luncheon, a stylish tea, or a lavish dinner dance, food is at the heart of the hospitality you extend to your guests. Your menu needs to be well planned, the food well prepared, and everything impeccably served—as we pride ourselves on at the Plaza. Here are our suggestions for the perfect fare to fit your occasion.

PANTRY COOK
PEDRO

CHEF GARDE-MANGER ERIC

EXECUTIVE CHEF
BRUNO TISON

SOUP CHEF LUÍS

Hot Hors D'Oeuvres

———

Honey-glazed Shrimp

Grilled Lamb Chops with Rosemary

Roulade of Veal and Tuna with Scallions

Plaza Crab Cakes with Tartar Sauce

Seasonal Miniquiches

Garlic Sausage en Croute

Chicken Sate with Peanut Sauce and Coconut

Coulibiac of Salmon

Wild Mushroom Feuilletés

Oysters Rockefeller

Gratinéed Crabmeat on Mushroom Caps

Spinach and Feta Cheese in Phyllo

Sautéed New York Foie Gras en Brioche

Honey-glazed shrimp

Coulibiac of salmon

Grilled lamb chops

Spinach triangles and mushroom feuilletés

Chicken sate

Sautéed foie gras

Oysters Rockefeller

All Photographs by Lou Manna

Cold Hors D'Oeuvres

Baked New Potato with Sevruga Caviar

Gravlox Canapé with Fresh Dill

Buffalo Mozzarella and Sun-dried Tomato on Baguette

Roquefort Napoleon

Scallop and Sea Bass Tartare in Clam Shell

Feuilleté of Shrimp Remoulade

Medallion of Lobster with Salmon Eggs

Smoked Mussels Croustade

Truffled Foie Gras on Toast

Blinis with Caviar

Roulade of Smoked Duck Breast and Duck Liver Mousse

Artichoke Heart with Spicy Salsa

Cherry Tomato Filled with Goat Cheese and Niçoise Olive

Grilled Seasonal Baby Vegetables with Parsley Mousseline

Scottish Smoked Salmon on Pumpernickel

MUSSELS, DUCK, ROQUEFORT, AND LOBSTER

SEASONAL BABY VEGETABLES

TOMATO, SHRIMP REMOULADE

BLINIS WITH CAVIAR

TRUFFLED FOIE GRAS ON TOAST

ARTICHOKE HEARTS WITH SALSA

NEW POTATO WITH CAVIAR

ALL PHOTOGRAPHS BY LOU MANNA

Spring Menus

LUNCH

Marinated Deep-Fried Bell Peppers with
Water Buffalo Mozzarella and
Opal Basil Vinegar

Atlantic Salmon en Croute with Vermouth
Chive Beurre Blanc

Wedding Cake

Migniardises and Coffee

Opposite: Lou Manna

DINNER

Terrine of Grilled Porcini and Portobello Mushrooms
in Red Bell Pepper Emulsion with Chive Oil
Bermuda Onion Compote

Roast Rack of Spring Lamb with Sage and
Rosemary
Seasonal Baby Vegetables
Pommes Boulangere

Blueberry Soufflé with Blueberry Coulis

Plaza Wedding Cake

Long-Stem Chocolate Strawberries
and Migniardises

Coffee and Assorted Teas

Opposite: Lou Manna

Summer Menus

LUNCH

Chilled Vichyssoise with a Lemon Snowball
and Russian Beluga Caviar

Amish Farm-Raised Chicken with
Crayfish Sauce, Stuffed Summer Squash,
and Tomato Rice

Washington State Granny Smith Apple Granité

Wedding Cake

Migniardises and Coffee

DINNER

Layered Applewood Smoked Salmon with
Osetra Caviar and Dill Crème Fraîche
Toasted Sourdough Baguette

Beef Tournedos with Sautéed New York
Foie Gras in Black Truffle Sauce
Pommes Parisienne
Bouquet of French Green Beans
Corn-Stuffed Tomato

Poached White Peach on Sauternes Jelly
with Pistachio Mousse and Anise Biscotti

Plaza Wedding Cake

Glazed White Figs and Migniardises

Coffee and Assorted Teas

Fall Menus

LUNCH

Game Consommé with Foie Gras Profiteroles

Poached Dover Sole in Lettuce,
Black Truffle Fumet with Honey Cap Mushrooms,
and California Green Asparagus

Wedding Cake

Migniardises and Coffee

DINNER

Autumn Wild Mushroom Risotto

Seared Venison Chops and Noisettes with
Sauce Poivrade and Poached Seckel Pears
Butternut Squash Custard
Pommes Château
Glazed Carrots and Turnips

Frozen Tangerine Mousse with Blackberry Coulis

Stilton with Old Port and Toasted Raisin-Walnut Bread

Plaza Wedding Cake

Caraibes Chocolate Truffles and Migniardises

Coffee and Assorted Teas

Winter Menus

LUNCH

SEARED TUNA LOIN AND SMOKED SCALLOPS WITH
MESCLUN IN CARDAMOM SHALLOT VINAIGRETTE

ROAST FREE-RANGE TURKEY WITH NATURAL JUICE
POMMES GAUFRETTES
CRANBERRY-STUFFED PEACHES
YELLOW TURNIP PUREE

WEDDING CAKE

MIGNIARDISES AND COFFEE

OPPOSITE: LOU MANNA

DINNER

Rosace of Maine Lobster and
Saffroned Turnip
Sevruga Caviar in a Blinis Crêpe

Fowl Consommé with Quenelles of Pheasant

Braised Loin of Veal with Oregon Morel Cream
Wild Rice with Pignoli Nuts
Yellow and Green Zucchini
Sautéed Spinach

Winter Baby Lettuce with Whole Grain Mustard
Walnut Dressing
Selected Farmer Cheeses
Stone-Baked Semolina Bread

Plaza Wedding Cake

Macerated Grapefruit and Orange Rings
and Migniardises

Coffee and Assorted Teas

Opposite: Lou Manna

Plaza Brunch
from Our Cold Buffet

FRESHLY SHUCKED OYSTERS AND CLAMS WITH
SHALLOT VINEGAR OR COCKTAIL SAUCE

JUMBO SHRIMP ON ICE

SCOTTISH SMOKED SALMON WITH
PUMPERNICKEL BREAD

POACHED HALIBUT WITH ROASTED PEPPERS

TOMATO AND WATER BUFFALO MOZZARELLA WITH
BALSAMIC VINEGAR

PARMA PROSCIUTTO AND SEASONAL MELON

DUCK, TURKEY, AND FOIE GRAS BALLOTTINE WITH
ONION CHUTNEY

TRICOLORE VEGETABLE TERRINE

EGGPLANT CUSTARD TERRINE

SALMON AND BOSTON SOLE TERRINE WITH
WATERCRESS SAUCE

LOBSTER AND TARRAGON TERRINE

SMOKED EEL, SMOKED TROUT, SMOKED SCALLOPS,
SMOKED BLUEFISH AND CONDIMENTS WITH
CREAM CHEESE AND ASSORTED BAGELS

Breakfast Breads and Pastries

FRENCH BRIOCHES AND CROISSANTS

ASSORTED DANISH

BLUEBERRY, CORN BANANA, AND BRAN MUFFINS

CHOCOLATE AND RAISIN PETITS PAINS

COFFEE CAKE BREAD

CHAMPAGNE MASCARPONE CAKE

BRAZILIAN MOUSSE WITH COFFEE SYRUP

CHOCOLATE MARQUISE

SICILIAN PISTACHIO AND MANDARIN ORANGE MOUSSE

APPLE-WALNUT MACAROON TARTE

CHOCOLATE MUD PIE WITH PECANS

PLAZA CHEESE CAKE

FROZEN TANGERINE MOUSSE

CRÊPES SUZETTE

WARM PEACH COBBLER

OPPOSITE: FRED MARCUS

Plaza Brunch
from Our Hot Buffet

OUR SELECTION OF OMELETS MADE TO ORDER:
MUSHROOM, BELL PEPPER, CRAB, SHRIMP,
SMOKED SALMON, ONION, HAM, CAVIAR, AND
CHEDDAR CHEESE

PORCINI TRIANGOLINI PRIMAVERA

CASSEROLE OF LOBSTER AND SWORDFISH THERMIDOR

POACHED EGGS BENEDICT

CARVED RACK OF VEAL WITH OREGON MOREL CREAM

BRAISED FREE-RANGE CHICKEN WITH GREEN OLIVE,
ASPARAGUS, AND EGGPLANT

ROAST FILET MIGNON OF BEEF IN PINOT NOIR SAUCE

GRATIN DAUPHINOISE

STUFFED ARTICHOKE WITH ACORN SQUASH PURÉE

VEGETABLE JARDINIÈRE AND WILD MUSHROOM RISOTTO

BELGIAN WAFFLES AND CHERRY, APPLE, AND
LEMON BLINTZES WITH WHIPPED CREAM AND
MAPLE SYRUP

Recipes

BLUEBERRY SOUFFLÉ WITH BLUEBERRY COULIS

SERVES 4

PASTRY CREAM
 1 quart milk
 ½ cup plus 1½ tablespoons cornstarch
 1 cup plus 1½ tablespoons sugar
 3 eggs
 2 egg yolks
 6½ tablespoons butter

COULIS
 2 cups blueberries
 2½ tablespoons sugar

BLUEBERRY PURÉE
 2 cups blueberries
 4 teaspoons sugar

 4 egg yolks
 6½ egg whites
 ¼ cup fresh blueberries
 1 tablespoon confectioners' sugar

Make the pastry cream: Heat 3 cups of the milk until warm. In a small bowl, dissolve the cornstarch in the remaining cup of milk. In a large bowl, combine the sugar, eggs, and egg yolks and mix well. Add the warm milk to the egg mixture, then add the milk with the cornstarch. Transfer to a 2-quart saucepan, place over medium heat, and slowly bring to a boil, constantly stirring to avoid burning at the bottom. Add the butter before the pastry cream starts to thicken. When it has thickened, remove from the heat and strain.

Make the blueberry coulis: In a food processor, purée the blueberries with the sugar. Strain.

Make the blueberry purée: In a small saucepan, cook the blueberries and sugar until reduced to a thick purée. You should obtain ¾ cup to 1 cup purée.

Assemble and bake the soufflé: Preheat the oven to 400° F. Butter and sugar four 7-ounce soufflé molds. Mix the pastry cream, the blueberry purée, and the 4 egg yolks together. Whip the egg whites to medium stiffness. With a rubber spatula, carefully fold the egg whites into the pastry cream/purée mixture, and then fold the ¼ cup fresh blueberries into this mixture. Pour into the prepared soufflé molds and bake for about 20 to 25 minutes, until golden brown.

When done, remove the soufflé from the oven, sprinkle the top with confectioners' sugar, and serve immediately, passing the coulis separately in a small pitcher.

Washington State Granny Smith Apple Granité

Note that for this granité, the apple cubes have to be stored in the freezer overnight.

SERVES 4

2 large or 3 small Granny Smith apples
½ cup sugar
⅞ cup water
Juice of 1 lemon

Rinse the apples. Cut them into 1-inch cubes, leaving the skin on and removing the core, and store in the freezer overnight.

The next day, place the sugar and water in a small saucepan, bring to a boil, remove from the heat, and allow to cool.

Put the diced apples in a blender, pour the cooled syrup over the apples, and add the lemon juice. Blend to a purée.

Put the purée in an ice cream maker and follow manufacturer's instructions for freezing.

Blinis with Caviar

¾ cup cake flour
1 cup bread flour
Pinch of salt
¼ teaspoon baking soda
4 eggs, separated
1 tablespoon vegetable oil
1½ cups milk
Caviar
Crème fraîche or sour cream (optional)
Lemon (optional)

Place the cake flour and the bread flour in a large bowl. Place the salt and baking soda around the edges of the flour. In the center, pour the egg yolks and oil. Then start to pour the milk slowly and mix the ingredients at the same time. Mix until just blended.

In a medium bowl, whip the egg whites to stiff peaks and fold into the first mixture with a rubber spatula.

Add some oil to a blini pan or other large pan and start making 1½-inch crêpes. Keep the blinis warm in a 200° F. oven while you finish the rest.

Serve with caviar. If using pressed caviar, serve with crème fraîche or sour cream. Place a small amount of crème fraîche on each blini, then top with some caviar. Lemon could also be served for those who prefer it. Vodka or champagne is the perfect beverage with blinis.

Chilled Vichyssoise with a Lemon Snowball and Russian Beluga Caviar

Serves 12

4 tablespoons butter
1 onion, sliced very thin
2 leeks, sliced very thin
1 garlic clove, sliced very thin
2 celery stalks, sliced very thin
2 quarts chicken stock
4 medium potatoes, peeled and sliced
Salt
2 cups heavy cream
2 bunches chives, chopped
freshly ground black pepper (to taste)
Tabasco (to taste)
1 Lemon Snowball (recipe follows)
12 ounces beluga caviar

In a large kettle or stockpot, heat the butter and cook the onion, leeks, garlic, and celery slowly until soft and translucent. Add the chicken stock. Simmer for 30 minutes and then add the potatoes. Season lightly with salt. Cook until all the vegetables are tender, then purée the soup in a food processor. Chill well. When the soup is cold, stir in the cream and chopped chives. Correct the salt and add pepper and Tabasco to taste. Serve cold in a chilled tureen, float the Lemon Snowball in the tureen, and pass the beluga caviar.

Lemon Snowball

6 egg whites
Pinch of salt
Juice of ½ lemon

Whip the egg whites with the salt and lemon juice until stiff peaks form. Shape the egg whites into a slightly flattened round or oval form and cook over medium heat in a bain-marie, or other vessel suitable for poaching the snowball, for 2 minutes on each side. Chill well. Serve cold, floating in the vichyssoise tureen.

Terrine of Grilled Porcini and Portobello Mushrooms in Red Bell Pepper Emulsion with Chive Oil

This terrine must be made the day before you plan to serve it, since it has to remain in the refrigerator, weighted, overnight.

MARINATED MUSHROOMS

3 pounds large portobello mushrooms

3 pounds large porcini mushrooms

2 cups olive oil

3 garlic cloves, crushed

2 sprigs fresh rosemary

WILD MUSHROOM CREAM

6 leaves gelatin

2 pounds wild mushrooms, such as shiitake or morel

6 tablespoons butter

4 large shallots, chopped (about 1¼ cups)

Salt and freshly ground pepper

1 quart heavy cream

10 whole eggs

CHIVE OIL

1 cup olive oil

6 bunches of chives

TO ASSEMBLE THE TERRINE

4 leaves gelatin

Red Bell Pepper Emulsion (recipe follows)

*M*arinate the portobellos and porcinis: Clean and wash the portobellos. Remove the dark side of the cap. Do the same with the porcinis. Separate the caps from the stems and marinate both caps and stems in 2 cups olive oil with the crushed garlic and the rosemary. For added flavor, half of the rosemary can be chopped. When the mushrooms have marinated for 1 hour, grill each piece of mushroom until nicely browned, or broil under a broiler. Let cool.

Make the wild mushroom cream: Soak the gelatin for the wild mushroom cream and the gelatin for assembling the terrine (10 leaves altogether) in cold water for 20 minutes. Clean and wash the wild mushrooms. Heat the butter and sauté the mushrooms with the shallots until the mushroom liquid has evaporated and the shallots are translucent. Season with salt and pepper to taste. Add the cream and bring to a boil. Reduce slightly, then remove from the heat and allow to cool. When completely cooled, add the eggs and 6 leaves of gelatin. Process the mushroom cream in a blender and then pass it through a fine chinois.

Make the chive oil: Place the 1 cup of oil and the chives in a blender. Process until smooth and strain through a piece of cheesecloth.

Preheat the oven to 350° F. Butter the terrine and start to mold the ingredients into the terrine. Start with a layer of porcinis and portobellos, using one-fifth of the mushrooms. Place a leaf of gelatin over the mushrooms and pour one-fourth of the wild mushroom cream over the gelatin. Add another layer of porcinis and portobellos, and continue layering in this manner, ending with a layer of mushrooms.

Cover with aluminum foil and cook in the oven in a bain-marie for 45 minutes.

Press the terrine lightly for one night in the refrigerator.

When ready to serve, unmold and slice. Serve drizzled with the chive oil and the red bell pepper emulsion.

Red Bell Pepper Emulsion

5 large ripe red bell peppers
2 tablespoons Dijon mustard
1 to 2 tablespoons tomato paste
6 egg yolks
¼ cup red wine vinegar
Salt and cayenne pepper
3 cups extra-virgin olive oil

Rinse the bell peppers and remove the stem, core, and seeds. Slice thinly. Place in a blender with the mustard, tomato paste, egg yolks, and vinegar, and add salt and cayenne to taste. Blend until smooth, then incorporate olive oil slowly. Continue blending until mixture is pale red; adjust seasoning to taste. Pass through a fine chinois.

Serve with the terrine of grilled mushrooms.

Amish Farm-Raised Chicken with Crayfish Sauce, Stuffed Summer Squash, and Tomato Rice

Serves 4

1 Amish farm-raised chicken, 2½ to 3 pounds
16 crayfish
Salt and freshly ground pepper
¼ pound butter
2 tablespoons cognac
1 cup chicken stock
2 cups heavy cream
1 small (¾-ounce) black truffle, cut in julienne
1 sprig of fresh chervil

Clean the chicken and quarter it (you can ask your butcher to clean and quarter it for you).

In salted boiling water, cook the crayfish for about 7 minutes. Refresh in cold water. Separate the heads from the tails. Clean the tails and reserve both heads and tails.

Preheat the oven to 350° F.

Salt and pepper each chicken piece on both sides. In a large skillet with a cover, heat 4 tablespoons of the butter and sauté the chicken until the skin is crisp and golden brown. Remove the butter, replace it with 4 tablespoons of fresh butter, cover the skillet, and cook the chicken in the oven for 18 to 20 minutes.

When the chicken is done, remove all excess grease from the pan. Add the crayfish heads and flambé with the cognac. Deglaze the pan with the chicken stock and reduce the stock to half its volume. Add the cream and cook for 2 to 3 minutes. Remove the crayfish heads, add the crayfish tails, and reduce the sauce to the desired consistency.

Transfer the chicken, crayfish tails, and sauce to a plate and sprinkle with the black truffle julienne and fresh chervil.

Stuffed Summer Squash

8 baby summer squash
1 small Spanish onion
1 red pepper
2 tablespoons olive oil

Scrub the squash. Trim off both ends. Set 4 squash aside. Cut four squash into very fine dice.

Peel the onion. Cut into very fine dice. Remove the core and seeds from the red pepper. Cut into very fine dice.

Heat the olive oil in a sauté pan. Sauté the diced vegetables over medium heat for 2 minutes.

Slice the remaining squash lengthwise and scoop out the middles. Fill with the cooked vegetables.

Bake in a 350° oven until the zucchini is cooked, approximately 10 minutes.

Tomato Rice

¼ cup olive oil
1 cup diced tomato
3 tablespoons chopped onion
1 cup white rice
2½ cups water
1 bouquet garni (bay leaf, thyme, parsley stems)
4 tablespoons butter
Salt and freshly ground pepper

Preheat the oven to 350° F.

In a large ovenproof casserole, heat the olive oil and sauté the tomato and onion. Add the rice and cook, stirring, for about 3 to 4 minutes. Add the water, the bouquet garni, and the butter. Season with salt and pepper to taste. Cover and bake for 18 to 20 minutes. Remove bouquet garni and check seasoning.

Plaza Crab Cakes with Tartar Sauce

1 egg
½ cup mixed chopped fresh herbs, including parsley, chives, tarragon, coriander, and oregano
1 teaspoon Old Bay seasoning
1 tablespoon Dijon mustard
½ cup homemade mayonnaise
¼ cup mixed diced red, yellow, and green bell peppers, blanched slightly
1 pound fresh crab meat
1 slice white bread, trimmed of crust and broken into crumbs
½ cup New England oyster crackers, crumbled

In a large bowl, combine the egg, chopped herbs, Old Bay seasoning, mustard, mayonnaise, and bell peppers. Mix in the crab meat and gradually add the bread crumbs and crumbled crackers until the mixture just holds together but is not too wet. Test consistency and seasoning of mixture by deep-frying or sautéing a little piece of crab cake. If mixture falls apart, add a little more bread crumbs or crackers. Set aside for an hour to let the bread absorb the moisture.

Preheat the oven to 350° F.

Shape the crab cakes to size with an ice cream scoop. Deep-fry or sauté to obtain a golden brown color, then cook in the oven for 5 minutes.

Serve with homemade tartar sauce.

LAYERED APPLEWOOD SMOKED SALMON WITH OSETRA CAVIAR AND DILL CRÈME FRAÎCHE

SERVES 20

6 sheets gelatin
1½ pounds applewood smoked salmon
Juice of 1 lemon
1 quart crème fraîche, whipped
1 bunch of chopped dill
4 ounces osetra caviar
Freshly ground white pepper
Sourdough baguettes (optional)
Lemon wedges (optional)

Soak the gelatin leaves for 15 to 20 minutes in cold water.

Slice the smoked salmon, then prepare your terrine mold by placing the first slices of smoked salmon in the terrine, covering the inside entirely. Leave about 2 inches of salmon hanging out of the mold—this will be used to seal the terrine.

Remove the gelatin from the water and place in a small saucepan. Add the lemon juice and melt the gelatin over low heat. Whip the crème fraîche to a soft peak, then add the melted gelatin and chopped dill. Mix to ensure the gelatin is evenly distributed through the crème fraîche. Gently stir in the caviar, taking care not to break the eggs. Add white pepper to taste.

Start layering the terrine, placing a layer of caviar cream over each layer of salmon and making the salmon layers 1 slice thick. When the terrine is filled, flip the smoked salmon that is hanging over the edge of the terrine so that it seals the terrine.

Serve with toasted sourdough baguettes and, if you wish, some lemon wedges.

POACHED DOVER SOLE IN LETTUCE BUTTER, BLACK TRUFFLE FUMET WITH HONEY CAP MUSHROOMS, AND CALIFORNIA GREEN ASPARAGUS

SERVES 4

4 Dover sole, about 22 ounces each, in fillet
Salt and freshly ground pepper
20 to 25 green asparagus
3 heads Boston lettuce
½ pound butter
1 cup dry white wine
1 cup dry vermouth
1 cup fish stock
3 cups heavy cream
1 tablespoon truffle juice
4 slices winter black truffle
1 ounce honey cap mushrooms

*F*illet the Dover sole and season with salt and pepper. Roll the fillets, skin side inside, and use a wooden toothpick to hold them together.

Peel the asparagus, cut them into pieces 4 or 5 inches long, and blanch in salted water. Refresh under cold water.

Rinse the heads of lettuce. Use only the greenest leaves. Blanch them in salted water, refresh under cold water, and press firmly to get all the water out. Process in a food processor with the butter to obtain a smooth lettuce butter. Pass the lettuce butter through a fine chinois.

Place the fillets in a pan with the white wine, vermouth, and stock. Poach the fillets for 3 to 5 minutes. Remove them from the pan and continue cooking to reduce the liquid to half its volume. Add the cream and reduce again. Finish the sauce with the lettuce butter. Add the truffle juice, sole, and asparagus. Let it boil, check the seasoning, and arrange on a serving plate. Garnish with the truffle slices and sprinkle a few honey cap mushrooms around the fillets.

AUTUMN WILD MUSHROOM RISOTTO

SERVES 10

PORCINI PASTE

½ *medium onion, chopped fine*

9 *large garlic cloves, chopped fine*

6 *tablespoons olive oil*

1½ *pounds porcini mushrooms, rehydrated*

Salt and freshly ground pepper

RISOTTO

2 *medium onions, chopped fine*

9 *large garlic cloves, chopped fine*

¾ *cup olive oil*

2 *pounds Arborio rice*

1 *bottle (750 ml) dry white wine*

12 *ounces dried morel mushrooms, rehydrated*

10 *ounces oyster mushrooms*

9 *ounces portobello mushrooms*

8 *ounces button mushrooms*

8 *ounces shiitake mushrooms*

7 *ounces cremini mushrooms*

Chicken stock

Salt and freshly ground pepper

2½ *tablespoons truffle juice*

2½ *cups grated Parmigiano-Reggiano (10 ounces)*

½ *pound butter*

½ *bunch Italian parsley*

*M*ake the porcini paste: Sauté the onion and garlic in olive oil. Add the porcini and sauté until the liquid from the mushrooms and onions has been released and partly reduced. Season to taste and purée in a food processor.

Make the risotto: Sauté the onion and garlic in the olive oil. Stir in the rice. Sauté over medium heat until the rice becomes the color of pearls. Add the white wine and reduce the liquid slightly. Add the mushroom purée. Stir over medium heat until it becomes the consistency of a paste. Add the morels, oysters, portobellos, buttons, shiitakes, and creminis. Add warm chicken stock, a ladle at a time, stirring constantly, over medium heat. Wait until each ladleful of stock is absorbed before adding the next. When half the stock has been added and absorbed, season lightly with salt and pepper. Add the truffle juice. Continue cooking and adding stock until all the stock has been added.

Finish with the Parmesan, the butter, and the chopped parsley. Adjust seasoning.

SEARED VENISON CHOPS AND NOISETTES WITH SAUCE POIVRADE AND POACHED SECKEL PEARS

SERVES 4

This dish must be started two days before you plan to serve it, since the pears must be macerated for 48 hours. One day before serving, the venison has to be placed in the marinade.

POACHED PEARS
  4 Seckel pears
  2 cups red Burgundy wine
  1 cinnamon stick
  7 tablespoons sugar (divided)
  3 to 4 tablespoons butter

MARINATED VENISON CHOPS AND NOISETTES
  Venison bones and scraps
  1 carrot
  1 onion
  2 celery stalks
  4 cups red Burgundy wine
  ½ cup cognac
  ½ cup olive oil
  1 tablespoon juniper berries
  1 tablespoon cracked black peppercorns
  1 bouquet garni (bay leaf, thyme, parsley stems)
  4 venison chops
  4 noisettes, 2 ounces each, of venison filet mignon

SAUCE POIVRADE
  3 tablespoons flour
  2 cups red Burgundy wine
  2 to 3 tablespoons butter
  Salt and freshly ground pepper
  ½ pound butter
  2 tablespoons cracked white and pink peppercorns
  3 to 4 tablespoons butter
  2 tablespoons sugar
  8 sprigs of chervil

*P*oach and macerate the pears: Peel the pears and poach them for 15 minutes in the 2 cups of red wine with the cinnamon stick and 5 tablespoons of the sugar. Then let the pears macerate, refrigerated, for at least 48 hours.

Marinate the venison: Chop the venison bones and scraps into small pieces. Dice the carrot, onion, and celery. Make a marinade of the 4 cups of wine, the cognac, the oil, the juniper berries, the black peppercorns, and the bouquet garni. Add the vegetables, the chopped bones and scraps, and the venison chops and noisettes. Marinate overnight in the refrigerator. The next day separate the marinade from the vegetables and venison scraps and bones. Set the chops and noisettes aside. Reserve the bouquet garni.

Make the Sauce Poivrade: Preheat the oven to 400° F. Roast the marinated bones and scraps of venison for 30 minutes, then add the vegetables and roast for 30 minutes more. The bones and vegetables will have a carmel color. This increases the sugar content of the vegetables. When everything is well roasted, stir in the flour and cook for a few more minutes. Deglaze the pan with the 2 cups of wine, add the bouquet garni from the marinade, and cook for about 2 hours, or until the sauce reaches a deep red, almost brown color. Pass the sauce through a fine chinois. Finish the sauce with 2 or 3 tablespoons of butter and check the seasoning.

Brown ½ pound butter in a large skillet. Sprinkle the venison chops and noisettes with the cracked pink and white peppercorns, add salt to taste, and sear on both sides in the brown butter.

Sauté the pears with 3 or 4 tablespoons of butter and the remaining 2 tablespoons of sugar to give them a nice caramelized color.

To serve, place one venison chop and one noisette on each plate with a little bit of sauce poivrade, a few sprigs of chervil, and a poached pear. Serve with the vegetable of your choice. At the Plaza, we often serve our venison with butternut squash custard, glazed turned carrots and turnips, and a few pommes de terre château (potatoes cut to look like large olives, sautéed in butter, and then roasted).

MARINATED DEEP-FRIED BELL PEPPERS WITH WATER BUFFALO MOZZARELLA AND OPAL BASIL VINEGAR

SERVES 4

Enough vegetable oil to deep-fry the bell peppers
2 red bell peppers
2 yellow bell peppers
2 green bell peppers
½ cup extra-virgin olive oil
3 tablespoons opal basil vinegar
12 slices water buffalo mozzarella
4 sprigs of fresh basil
Freshly ground pepper

Heat the oil in a deep fryer or deep, heavy skillet and deep-fry the bell peppers until the skin is dark brown, almost black. The darker the color, the easier they will peel. Under cold running water, peel the peppers clean. Cut each pepper lengthwise into four equal parts and remove the seeds and cores. Drain the peppers on paper towels.

Make a marinade of the olive oil and opal basil vinegar and marinate the peppers at room temperature for 1 hour.

To serve, set three slices of mozzarella on each individual plate with alternate colors of bell peppers. Pour some of the marinade over the cheese and peppers and place one sprig of basil on each plate. Pass a pepper mill.

Seating Plans

*I*f your reception features a sit-down dinner, a seating plan ensures that guests are not left to fend for themselves. Care should be taken that a balance is struck between seating relatives and old friends together and integrating guests who may not know anyone else invited. Give some thought to congenial pairings by trying, wherever possible, to match people with common interests or backgrounds. One need not keep all the guests of the bride's family on one side of the room and all the guests of the groom's family on the other. Interspersing the tables reinforces the idea that two families unite at a wedding.

THE BRIDE'S TABLE

The newlyweds sit at the center of their table with the groom on the bride's left. The maid of honor sits on the groom's left, the best man on the bride's right. Other attendants sit on either side, accompanied by husband, wife, escort, or guest. Men and women alternate.

The bridal table is traditionally served by waiters even if the food at the reception is served buffet style.

If the bridal party is too large to be comfortably accommodated at one table, the bride and groom and their honor attendants share the bride's table and a separate table is set up for the attendants.

For a couple that prefers to circulate, rather than take its place at a formal bride's table, a table large enough to seat all the attendants should be reserved so that the bride and groom have a place to sit down.

THE PARENTS' TABLE

The parents' table is generally made up of the parents of the bride and groom, grandparents, whoever performed the ceremony and his or her spouse, and the godparents. Seating centers around the mother of the bride as follows: her husband to her right, the mother of the groom to his right, the minister or rabbi to the bride's mother's left, and the others in whatever order she chooses. If there are more guests who belong at the parents' table than can be seated there, the bride's parents may host one table and the groom's parents another, each filling out the seats as they choose. The minister or rabbi is seated with the bride's parents unless he is a guest of the groom's parents.

Divorced parents of either the bride or groom are not usually seated at the same table; each has a table with his or her own special guests.

PLACE CARDS

FRED MARCUS

Gifts for Attendants

The bride's gifts to her maid of honor and attendants may be presented at the bridesmaids' luncheon, at the rehearsal dinner, or at another time. Gifts of jewelry inscribed with the bride and groom's initials and the wedding date are always appropriate, as are such keepsakes as cut-crystal powder boxes or perfume atomizers, silver picture frames, compacts, key rings, or ornamental boxes.

The groom generally gives his gift to his best man and each usher at the bachelor dinner or the rehearsal dinner. In addition to such gifts of jewelry as cuff links or tie pins, the groom may give belt buckles, wallets, stud boxes, pens, or cut-crystal decanters.

FRED MARCUS

FROM THE WEDDING OF MICHELLE LEBER AND MICHAEL ROBERTS

I go to all the weddings in the White and Gold Room

and I usually stay for the reception

There are absolutely nothing but rooms in The Plaza

Ooooooooooooooooooooo I absolutely love The Plaza

Where the Magic Begins: Plaza Weddings

Marla Maples / Donald Trump

Ｗhen your name is Donald Trump and you are about to marry one of the most stunning ladies around—and you just happen to own New York's most famous landmark hotel—nothing short of spectacular will do for your wedding.

More than one thousand guests attended the wedding that made the papers around the world. As the limousines pulled up to a specially erected tent covering the length of the hotel's front drive, a veritable Who's Who of notables emerged. Magnates of industry, politicians, society leaders, and movie stars passed before crowds police estimated at more than ten thousand people.

Guests entered the Fifth Avenue lobby to the strains of violins and a harp, proceeded to the adjacent Rose Room for a security check, and then were escorted to the Grand Ballroom.

Larry Atlas, of Atlas Floral Decorators, had created a sea of white and crystal. Guests mingled before the ceremony as violins, a cello, a bass,

Top Right: DONALD'S SISTERS ELIZABETH GRAU AND JUDGE MARYANNE TRUMP BARRY, BROTHER-IN-LAW JIM GRAU, AND HIDDEN, DONALD'S MOTHER, MARY
Right: LIVE BROADCASTS COVERED THE CROWDS OUTSIDE THE PLAZA HOPING TO SEE SOMETHING OF MARLA AND DONALD'S WEDDING.

FRED MARCUS

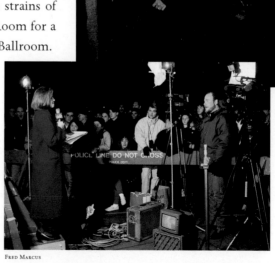

FRED MARCUS

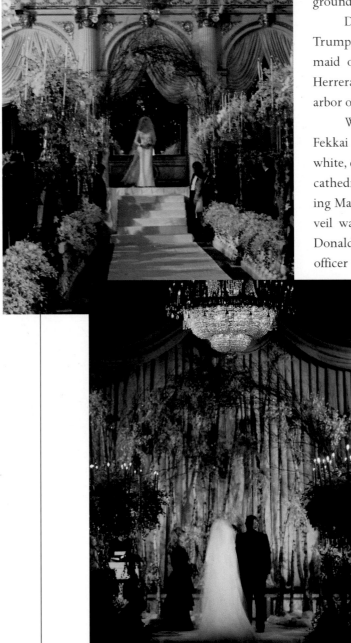

flutes, a harp, a piano, and chimes played softly in the background.

Donald Trump took his place with his father, Fred C. Trump, who was his best man, and Janie Elder, the bride's maid of honor, who wore a gown designed by Carolina Herrera. And then, from the center loge box, framed by an arbor of white birch trees and orchids, the bride appeared.

With hair and makeup by Frederic Fekkai of the Frederic Fekkai Beauty Center at Bergdorf Goodman, dressed in a white, double-faced satin, off-the-shoulder gown with double cathedral trains designed by Carolina Herrera, the breathtaking Marla Maples held all eyes. Shimmering above her bridal veil was a magnificent tiara of diamonds, compliments of Donald's longtime friend Ronald Winston, chief executive officer and president of Harry Winston. (Given just a week's notice, Winston and his chief designer, Ambaji Shinde, had sketched a selection of tiaras for the couple's approval. The choice made, the sketch was dispatched to the Winston Atelier, where expert jewelers worked around the clock to create the finished piece.) A flawless, 20-carat pear-shaped diamond formed a crest above 325 marquis-cut, pear-shaped, and brilliant-cut diamonds. (The following day, the tiara was returned to Mr. Winston.)

Marla was met at the base of the steps by her father, Stan Maples, who escorted her down an aisle bordered by white balustrades of similax vines and white orchids. On a raised platform covered with white birch trees, Reverend Arthur Caliandro, of Marble Collegiate Church, performed the ceremony. Camille Johnson of the Metropolitan Opera sang "The Lord's Prayer," and Louanne Gideon read from the Book of Prophets. A lingering embrace concluded the double-ring ceremony.

From the Grand Ballroom, the guests proceeded to the Terrace Room, whose doors had been opened to the Palm Court. A boxwood hedge with wrought-iron gates enclosed it. On satellite buffets interspersed throughout the two rooms, executive chef Bruno Tison had created a bounty that included gallatine of chicken with plums, terrine of duck with foie gras and pistachios, fish feuillette filled with trout and peppered mackerel, lobster montage with medallions of lobster, smoked Irish salmon, duck breast and smoked salmon, beluga caviar with blinis, rack of lamb, loin of tuna, and sushi bars. A sumptuous Viennese table held sugar pieces, croque en bouche, and miniature pastries. The food was accompanied by Louis Roederer Cristal champagne and Jordan wines of California.

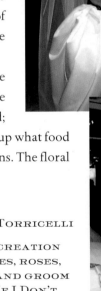

The pièce de résistance was a towering, nine-tier, eighty-inch-high creation by Sylvia Weinstock that comprised twenty individual cakes filled with chocolate mousse. The cake was covered in white frosting with sugar ivy vines and sugar roses, lilies, sweet peas, and freesia in ice blue, pale lavender, and white.

The bride and groom danced their first dance to "I Have Nothing If I Don't Have You" from *The Bodyguard.* Mark Stevens, of the Hank Lane Orchestra, and a twelve-piece band provided the music.

Nor were the invited guests the only recipients of the Trumps' hospitality. The happy groom and his lovely bride generously saw to it that their personal bounty was not wasted; at the close of the celebration, trucks from City Harvest picked up what food was left to distribute to a senior citizens' center and soup kitchens. The floral decorations were sent to hospitals around the city.

Left: BIANCA JAGGER AND REPRESENTATIVE ROBERT TORRICELLI

Top Right: SYLVIA WEINSTOCK'S EIGHTY-INCH-HIGH CREATION COVERED IN WHITE FROSTING WITH SUGAR IVY VINES, ROSES, LILIES, SWEET PEAS, AND FREESIA. *Center Right:* BRIDE AND GROOM DANCED THEIR FIRST DANCE TO "I HAVE NOTHING IF I DON'T HAVE YOU." MARK STEVENS, OF THE HANK LANE ORCHESTRA, AND A TWELVE-PIECE ORCHESTRA PROVIDED THE MUSIC.

THIS PAGE AND PAGES 148–149: FRED MARCUS PHOTOGRAPHY / ANDY MARCUS, PHOTOGRAPHER

FRED MARCUS

Perri Peltz / Eric Ruttenberg

Perri Peltz, weekend news anchor for WNBC, met Eric Ruttenberg through her brother, Harlan Peltz. They started dating while Perri was still an on-camera reporter for WNBC. (They continued dating, Perri claims, because Eric overwhelmed her with his willingness to meet her wherever and whenever her stories took place, including in the Bronx at eleven o'clock for a dog story.)

Once they became engaged, the couple had their hearts set on a garden wedding in June. The bride's mother, however, had some trepidation about trusting to weather that was outside her control. As a hostess and chairperson of such events as Opening Night at Carnegie Hall and the Irvington Institute's Annual Kitchen Caper at the Four Seasons, Lauren Veronis is no stranger to lavish functions—and their pitfalls. Rather than risk fickle weather, she and the bride and groom decided to bring the garden indoors—to the Plaza.

The wedding ceremony itself was held at the Park Avenue Synagogue. Derald Ruttenberg, the groom's father, served as his best man. The bride came down the aisle, escorted by her stepfather, John Veronis, in a gown of re-embroidered white cotton lace designed by Carolyne Roehm. An off-the-shoulder cotton lace collar rested at the shoulder line, topping a long-sleeved, dropped-waist, fitted bodice. The edges of the collar, bodice, and sleeves were scalloped. The bouffant skirt's detachable cathedral train, scalloped around the edges, was caught at the center back by a self-bow. On her head the bride wore a lace band anchoring a cathedral-length, white silk tulle veil.

Perri's attendants also wore gowns designed by Carolyne Roehm. White satin-faced organza blouses with tailored shirt collars and full poet's sleeves topped softly gathered full skirts of satin-faced organza—aquamarine for Perri's sister, Alexandra Peltz, maid of honor; and for Mrs. Elizabeth Close, matron of honor; and peach for attendants Jane Veronis, Perri's stepsister; and Hattie and Kathy Ruttenberg, Eric's sisters. The skirts' hems reached to the ankle at center front and to the floor at center back. Pistachio green duchess satin sashes completed the ensembles.

Four flower girls, nieces of the bride and groom and children of close friends, wore Carolyne Roehm peony-pink taffeta ballerina-length dresses with lace and organdy

Opposite: EACH TIER OF SYLVIA WEINSTOCK'S CAKE WAS NEARLY A FOOT HIGH AND HAD LACE ICING SURROUNDED BY BASKETS OF SPUN SUGAR ROSES, LILY OF THE VALLEY, AND PALE GREEN HYDRANGEA.

ruffs and hand-pleated bodices. Pleating on the outer tier of the double-layered skirts matched the bodices; the hems of the balloon sleeves and the double-tiered petticoats were trimmed in lace and tulle.

At the close of the wedding ceremony, guests left the Park Avenue Synagogue for the Plaza. Entering through the Palm Court, they gathered for a cocktail reception in the Terrace Room, transformed for the evening into a glorious English garden. Ivy cascaded from the walls. The columns were uplighted, creating a soft romantic glow that accentuated the architecture and the greenery. The balustrade bays were strung with ivy and lit by pillar candles of varying sizes. Pots of blooming garden roses, lily, and astilbe graced the area. The feeling was enhanced by eight-foot-tall privet trees arching from each level of the Terrace Room's "garden."

Leaving the Terrace Room, guests arrived at the Grand Ballroom—and stepped into a Florentine courtyard. Ivy draped the walls from ceiling to floor and ivy drapes covered the doorways. Plum and tea rose striped sovereign moiré cloths covered the tables and were complemented by bronze ballroom chairs with burgundy seats. To carry through the theme of a garden wedding held at home, each unique centerpiece incorporated antique family heirlooms from the bride's home. These were filled with an overflowing array of white garden roses accented with vibrantly colored strawberries, gooseberries, currants, apricots, black grapes, and ivy. The bridal table was covered with an antique lace cloth from the bride's grandmother, Mrs. Rae Nelson. Designer Robert Isabell coordinated all aspects of the decor with Mrs. Veronis.

For the nuptial dinner, Mrs. Veronis requested a perfectly prepared, reasonably simple meal. The Plaza chef served penne with fresh truffles (shaved at table, the truffles gave off an incredible aroma). This was followed by roasted baby turkey, spring vegetables, pommes gaufrettes, and cranberries and peaches. (Mrs. Veronis laid particular stress on questions of serving: The meal was to be served as though the guests were in a fine home with an impeccable butler.)

Sylvia Weinstock's magnificent wedding cake boasted five tiers, each nearly a foot high, with lace icing surrounded by baskets of spun sugar roses, lily of the valley, and pale green hydrangea.

Throughout dinner, four Gypsy violins played soft, romantic music; then, just prior to dessert, the violins gave way to Mark Stevens of the Hank Lane Orchestra. With twelve musicians and three vocalists, the stage was set for nonstop dancing.

And not a hint of rain to spoil the evening.

Lisa Aitken / Dr. David Desmond

*E*ven if Donald Trump *weren't* his uncle, Dr. David Desmond says with a smile, he would still have wanted to have his wedding at the Plaza. Happily, Lisa Aitken concurred.

From the first, everything about the look and atmosphere of the hotel convinced her it was the perfect place for the wedding she and David wanted. She was not disappointed.

David, who concedes that most of the planning was left to Lisa—"I just showed up and had a great time"—did his best to help.

"I proposed to Lisa with only one proviso: that she not *think* about planning a wedding for three months, just so she could relax and enjoy being engaged," he says. "Within one week, it was all set up." Brushing aside Lisa's soft demur, he repeats firmly, "Within one week."

It's Lisa's turn to smile. Even with an M.B.A. and experience handling special events for a major corporation, she can testify it wasn't quite that expeditious. But she did know what she wanted. Having grown up in a series of exotic locales ranging from Venezuela to Sydney, Australia; Djakarta, Indonesia; Singapore; and Canton, China—not to mention her university years in Texas—Lisa wanted a very traditional wedding.

She could see it. A beautiful church service followed by a reception and dinner dance. A guest list that would allow for time with everyone gathered. An intimate, sit-down dinner, and music that would bring the crowd to its feet.

Throughout, every detail was thoughtfully executed, the choices reflecting the particular elegant simplicity that is hers.

FRED MARCUS

For their ceremony the couple chose St. Thomas Episcopal on Fifth Avenue. Long known for its splendid music program (and generations of fashionable weddings), the magnificent interior provided the setting for the groom's most vivid wedding memory: "When I saw Lisa walking in the door of the church, I was suddenly struck by my absolute conviction that this was the woman for me. I'd known it before, but not with such clarity and force. I thought how wonderful to have this realization, in this place, at this moment."

Dressed in an off-white, hand-beaded Carolina Herrera gown, Lisa carried a bouquet of roses—"very simple, very full, all open." Her

CAKE BY SYLVIA WEINSTOCK

attendants were also dressed in off-white, the color scheme for the wedding.

The bride's most memorable moment was the first dance as husband and wife, as the band played "It Had to Be You." With Hank Lane himself providing the music (along with a string quartet to fill in during the band's breaks), few guests had to be coaxed to join the bridal couple on the dance floor. The timing and intensity of the music dovetailed perfectly with the table service, a triumph of coordination between Hank Lane and the Plaza's incomparable executive director of banquets, Paul Nicaj.

In the Grand Ballroom, where the dinner was held, Lisa felt little was needed in the way of additional adornment. She chose off-white linens, draped and gathered in rosettes, for her tables. The centerpieces—all roses in pastel colors—matched the floral pattern of the china. Candles on each table provided an atmosphere of warmth and intimacy.

Sylvia Weinstock's cake matched the decor. "It was so beautiful I wished we didn't have to cut into it," Lisa confessed. "But it was delicious. I took the top home and froze it. On our first anniversary I served it with champagne." And how was it? one asks. There is a long pause. "Dreadful," Lisa finally admits. "I forgot to take it out in time."

"For the sake of tradition she made me have frozen cake and champagne," David says. "It was romantic in *concept*."

Elisa Cresci / Timothy McEvoy

When Nancy and Laurence Cresci's daughter, Elisa, became engaged to Tim McEvoy, they offered her a choice: Did she want to take twenty-five or thirty friends to Vail for two weeks and have a ceremony and party there; would she rather have the money; or did she want the fairy-tale wedding?

Elisa never hesitated for a moment. "As long as I can remember," she says, smiling, "I always had a vision of my wedding."

With characteristic decisiveness and her mother's undivided attention and wholehearted commitment to the project (not to mention a few expert contributions from her restaurateur father), Elisa plunged happily into the task of planning the wedding of her dreams.

For all three, the key was choosing the right location. "Once you find the place," says Nancy, "which, in my book, will always be the Plaza, you're in secure hands. You know that the choices and requests you make are going to be executed perfectly. The staff is your ally."

Nancy found herself relying confidently on the staff's advice for matters outside her purview. "We took a lot of their recommendations," she recalls. "After all, we were at the Plaza—they weren't going to recommend people who weren't good."

As owners of New York's Manhattan Café, Nancy and Larry had a head start when it came to questions of party decor, presentation, and cuisine. As doting parents, they wanted to pull out all the stops and make an unforgettable wedding for their only child. As a family, the trio were in agreement over the essential question of style. That helped; they are clearly three individuals with very strongly held opinions.

"I am not an indecisive person," Elisa notes. As a working actress who takes an active role in her parents' restaurant,

FRED MARCUS

OPPOSITE: FRED MARCUS

she brought her own flair for drama to a background that recognized and valued good taste. And she is refreshingly clear on matters pertaining to herself: "I know what I want."

In this case, what she wanted was a personalized version of a traditional wedding—one that had an Old World feel but bore her unmistakable stamp. It wasn't a question of being different for difference's sake; her purpose was quite specific. For Elisa, the essence of the wedding lay in gathering friends and family around her to witness a momentous step in her life. Therefore, what mattered most were her guests. The hospitality they were offered must reflect how much they meant to her and to her family.

Not a single detail was overlooked. Every aspect— from custom-made velvet wraps for the bridesmaids to tiny gold envelopes disguising packets of sweetener at the tables—was given attention. Great trouble was taken over amenities and favors.

Given the welter of details, Elisa was careful to retain a sense of the wedding as a whole. From the first she viewed the wedding not as an isolated event but as the culmination of an event that began with the engagement. Maintaining a sense of continuity and seeing to it that everything fit together and enhanced the whole was critical to her.

To Nancy, who relished the experience as much as her daughter, the process was fairly straightforward. "We had the guidelines on what to do and then we took things a couple of steps further: We put in a lot of our own feelings and thoughts, we absorbed people's suggestions, and in the end, we created something that was different."

With everything done with such a lavish hand, the task was gargantuan; but apart from their enthusiasm, one clear advantage the family had was their ability to approach each aspect in a professional manner.

Above: MR. AND MRS. LAURENCE CRESCI.

Above: ELISA AND HER
MOTHER, NANCY.

Right: GIFT BAGS
FILLED WITH
MEMENTOS FOR THE
GUESTS.

FRED MARCUS

"We took direction from people who knew what they were doing," Nancy says firmly. "You're dealing with creative people; you want to give them your input and you want them to take that input, expand upon it, and make it better. That's why you've gone to them in the first place. If you could do better, you'd be doing it for a living." She's aware of the price one pays for being intractable. "If you go in with the attitude that 'It's my way or the highway'—you'll end up with something mediocre."

Elisa concurs. "Nothing anyone had to offer was ignored or dismissed out of hand. Knowing what you want doesn't mean being closed to other opinions, it means having confidence in the decision you finally make."

The wedding was a triumph of foresight and imagination. And as Elisa says happily, "It was nice to dream something like that for so many years and then be given the chance to live it."

Lisa Feinberg / Eric Blumencranz

When it came to weddings, Lisa Feinberg had some distinct advantages: As personal assistant to George Grisco, of the Plaza's legendary Atlas Floral Decorators, she'd had an opportunity to work on many of New York's most stylish weddings. And when it came to her own wedding, she was not at a loss. As she says with a smile, "I've known what I wanted since I was five years old."

What she wanted was something grand, something with the ambience of those wonderful old black-and-white movies she'd watched late at night. She wanted to feel as though she'd stepped out of time and back into an era where F. Scott Fitzgerald's Gatsby and Daisy might have felt welcome.

So when the time came to plan her wedding, she knew exactly where to begin.

"If I had to pick one place, it was the Plaza," Lisa says. Why? "Because it was the biggest and the most elegant, and I wanted something grand. I wanted an aisle with a long walk; I didn't

DENIS GARTNER

want that part to be over in a flash. And I wanted a room that made everyone who walked in feel it was straight out of another era."

In this Lisa had a staunch ally: her mother. "It really was always my dream to have my daughter married at the Plaza and have a very romantic wedding," acknowledges Judy Feinberg. For both, the look was the first priority.

"I wanted a lot of candles and I wanted a lot of flowers and I wanted it very luminous," says Lisa. "I didn't want any color—it was all very pale yellow and white." Mrs. Feinberg contributed some very definite ideas of her own. "My mother wanted green ivy *everywhere*," Lisa remembers. "She wanted the whole room dripping with ivy, so whatever flowers were used would drape downwards the way vines do. It was very effective."

To enhance her own ideas, Lisa took careful note of each Plaza wedding that she saw. She was such a familiar presence around the hotel that everyone called her "Eloise."

"I saw what was designed for others in the year I worked for Atlas and I would pick out bits and pieces, effects I particularly liked," she says. "George had done one wedding where there were little votive candles lining the whole room. I said, 'I have to have that.' And then at a different wedding, there were topiaries down the aisle and I said, 'I have to have topiaries.' Actually, more than what I did like, I got to know what I didn't like. George took that and came back with what I did like."

Lisa selected only those elements that would enhance the basic look she sought and be appropriate to a late summer wedding. "They transformed the room, there were candles every-where," Lisa says, describing the room in which the ceremony was held. "We used Casablanca lilies with yellow centers and big, pale yellow Bahama roses and lots of little orchids—it was mostly white, with touches of pale yellow, just to give it a little zest. And, thanks to my mother, there was a lot of rich, verdant green because everything was draped with ivy."

Lisa is quick to give credit to the extraordinary talents of her former boss. "I went to him and described my fantasy wedding—and he and the staff made it come true—they really did." It is clearly a memory she cherishes. "I wanted it to be the night I've dreamed of my whole life—and it was more. I wanted it to be something that in my wildest dreams I couldn't imagine actually happening for me, and it was."

Her mother smiles. "George was able to capture just what Lisa was going for, a certain dreamy, romantic look that was a masterpiece of understated elegance."

On everything, Lisa had the input of her fiancé, Eric Blumencranz. The ceremony was as carefully planned as the decor. "We had strong violins play-ing while everyone sat down and the music that they

Opposite Left: LISA ON THE ARM OF HER FATHER, JAY FEINBERG.

Denis Gartner

Denis Gartner

played before we walked in was all classical," Lisa recalls. "The whole thing was very old-fashioned; truly like something from another period. There were no updated songs." Lisa walked down the aisle to Pachelbel's Canon played very slowly and dramatically, over and over.

For the dinner dance, the same overall look was carried through. All the arrangements were taken from the Terrace Room and put into the Grand Ballroom, including the topiaries. The tables were swathed in an undercloth of gold and the overcloth was swagged up by rosettes. Every detail was perfect, right down to the pats of butter on the table—each rested on a little green leaf so they looked like little flowers. Everything went together.

DENIS GARTNER

The selection of the food had offered a particular pleasure to Lisa and her mother. "The most interesting thing about the Plaza, which I adored," says Mrs. Feinberg, "was the tasting menu they gave you ahead of time. Then you really get to taste everything."

"Not only was that good because you got to taste the food," says Lisa, "that is part of the experience of having your wedding at the Plaza. You go down into the bowels of the hotel, some basement or subbasement, and suddenly they open a door and there's the dining room. The chef himself comes in to speak with you about the food. And then, of course, you could taste all the desserts. We chose Baked Alaska and it was the most enormous success."

Mother and daughter are lavish in their praise for the staff, particularly Richard Pizzuto, assistant director of catering, and the incomparable Paul Nicaj, executive director of banquets. "They did a spectacular job," Mrs. Feinberg says unhesitatingly. "They know just *what* to do, they know just how to do it." And, Lisa interjects, "They made it fun. There was no pressure, no clash—they only wanted to accommodate me."

The cake, by Sylvia Weinstock, was a simple confection of tiers of chocolate chiffon and vanilla icing, at the groom's request. But there simplicity ended. In true Sylvia Weinstock fashion, the decorations took the guests' breath away.

"We told Sylvia a lot of the specific flowers that would be used in the floral arrangements," says Lisa. "All I can say is, the table had real flowers surrounding the cake. You could barely tell the difference between what was edible and what was not. Even knowing what was going into the cake and how many tiers and what flowers we'd asked for—when I walked in and saw it— I could not believe that was *my* cake."

Lisa feels she and Eric were very lucky; not only did the wedding look beautiful—everyone had a very good time. The dance floor was packed.

"Mark Stevens did the music," says Lisa. "I went in with a list of music—type of music, that is—and said, 'I want Motown and I want seventies disco and I want absolutely no Top 40 from today,' and that's what I got." Her first dance with her husband was to a song the orchestra had never done before—"More Than Words" by Extreme—they learned it just for the wedding. The song she danced to with her father was an original arrangement of tunes by the Beatles and Bette Midler.

If ever there was a radiant bride, it was Lisa Blumencranz. One doesn't doubt her for a moment when she says how much she savored her wedding. "I was so excited, so excited about it all. I felt this was my night and I was going to live it to the fullest. It far surpassed my wildest dreams."

Martha Kramer / Neal Jay Fox

Martha Kramer, who heads up Emanuel Ungaro's North American operations, and Neal Jay Fox, president of Sulka, Inc., had been dating for some time by December 1989. On the evening of the annual Costume Institute Gala at the Metropolitan Museum of Art—which coincidentally happened to be Neal's birthday—Neal came to Martha's apartment to escort her to the event. He handed her a small gift box from Cartier that he said he had received that day. Martha, who could not understand why Neal was giving her his birthday present, opened it—only to find an exquisite Cartier diamond engagement ring.

Neal kept asking, "Will you marry me?" but Martha, caught totally off guard, found herself almost too stunned to respond.

(Word has it that Martha's great friend Ivana Trump helped Neal select the diamond, but it is the Costume Institute Gala that the couple view as their real good luck charm. Each year they attend revives wonderful memories.)

On a beautiful, sunny third of June, Martha and Neal were married.

The informal ceremony, with nuptials performed by Rabbi Balfour Brickner, was held in the Plaza's State Suite. The couple stood before a gilded fireplace banked with peonies, orchids, roses, tulips, and lilies of the valley—a creation of noted florist Rinaldo Maia.

Wearing a dress Emanuel Ungaro had personally designed for her, Martha carried a bridal bouquet of lilies of the valley. The six children who served as her attendants were all in white with garlands of baby orchids in their hair.

The wedding was marked by the presence of a host of celebrities. Close friend Neil Sedaka serenaded the couple with

MARY HILLIARD

CECE KIESELSTEIN-CORD, NEIL SEDAKA BEING KISSED BY THE GROOM, MRS. RALPH LAUREN.

two of their favorite songs, "Laughter in the Rain" and "The Miracle Song." Society photographer Mary Hilliard, another close friend, covered the event.

Guests dined on chilled vichyssoise with beluga caviar, salmon en croute stuffed with lobster and mushrooms with a lobster beurre blanc sauce, and pencil-thin asparagus tips. (The salmon was fashioned in the shape of a whole salmon with the crust made to look as though the fish was smiling.) The beautiful Sylvia Weinstock cake, served with champagne truffles and Marshall strawberries dipped in chocolate, was accompanied by Perrier Jouet champagne. For the luncheon, the hotel's very special Oscar de la Renta china was used.

Laurie Ellen Lindenbaum / Robert Allan Horne

The candlelit warmth of the Terrace Room provided the setting for the nuptials of Laurie Ellen Lindenbaum and Robert Allan Horne, helping to carry on a tradition begun ten years before by the bride's sister Erica.

Mother of the bride, Linda Lindenbaum, was very clear about the atmosphere she wished to engender. First and foremost the wedding was to be a *party,* a wonderful celebration with nonstop dancing. Together with Laurie, who took part in the planning and decisions from the outset, Mrs. Lindenbaum wanted a tasteful, stylish party with a dreamy, softly lit ambience flattering to everyone in the room.

To create the background she sought, Mrs. Lindenbaum engaged Philip Baloun, of Philip Baloun Designs. She wanted a professional capable of reflecting her standards of taste and interpreting them in an original and striking fashion. She sought someone whose ideas would enhance her own and whose experience and expertise would ensure that the best choices had been made and that all decisions would be executed impeccably.

Many long hours of consultation went into deciding on the color scheme and arranging the perfect room. To enhance the ceiling without violating the integrity of its design, it was decorated with smilax garlands and festoons of white chiffon. The tables were covered in white moiré with deep green velvet flounced overlays caught up with matching velvet rosettes.

The bridesmaids all wore hunter green dresses.

Tall, four-branched silver candelabra were placed at the center of each table. Long white tapers rose from large bursts of white, pale peach, and claret roses mixed with white lilies and dendrobium orchids. Flowers were placed at the top and bottom of each candelabrum so guests could see across the table. The centerpieces created a striking look throughout the room and helped promote a feeling of warmth at each table as they did not impede conversation.

Fourteen large, nine-branched candelabra decorated with flowers and ivy stood in arches on both sides of the room.

A PLAZA WEDDING

Music was the second priority. To accommodate nonstop dancing, music had to be selected with great care. It had to be compelling enough to encourage guests onto the dance floor but not so loud and intrusive that it made conversation difficult. The Hank Lane Orchestra opened with a selection of Gershwin and Cole Porter tunes—a choice that bridged generations nicely and set an elegant tone—and moved into livelier numbers after dinner. With so many guests strangers to one another at weddings, Mrs. Lindenbaum felt that offering continuous dancing was a graceful way of keeping up the momentum of the evening.

Seating was handled with the same thoughtfulness. Guests fell into four basic groups: the bride's friends from high school and college and her colleagues from work; the bride's family, relatives, and family friends; the groom's school friends and work colleagues; and the groom's family, relatives, and family friends. The younger group and their friends were seated nearest the orchestra. The bride's and groom's guests were not exiled to separate sides of the room but were seated together, throughout, to encourage a more intimate, convivial atmosphere.

To ensure that the wedding toasts would not drag on awkwardly, the details of who would make them, and at what point in the evening, were worked out in advance. Although traditionally the best man proposes the first toast—followed by the groom, who replies with thanks and proposes a toast to his bride—in this case the first toast was offered by the bride's father, who was followed by the best man and the groom's father (often overlooked at weddings), respectively. The toasts were warm and sentimental—and, as all graceful toasts are, brief.

Mrs. Lindenbaum, anxious to avoid a big buffet that would be logistically difficult in a large crowd of people, had bite-size hors d'oeuvres passed by waiters throughout the reception. Guests were not kept waiting. The waiters appeared frequently and carried plates or napkins for discards.

The bride and her mother handled most of the arrangements as they were giving the party. Naturally, since the bridal *couple* was the focal point of the event, the groom was involved in the final site selection, the menu tasting prior to the reception, and the selection of the orchestra. The best man and the groomsmen were, as always, his responsibility.

The planning, the carefully thought-out arrangements, and the attention to detail resulted in what their guests unanimously attest to: an unforgettable wedding.

Carla Straniero / Dr. Robert Barone

Bright May sunshine provided a glorious backdrop for Carla Straniero Barone and Dr. Robert Barone as the hansom cab pulled up at the Plaza's portico with the bride and bridegroom. Their guests, having attended the beautiful nuptial mass at Park Avenue's St. Ignatius Loyola Church, were assembled outside to greet them.

Carla and Robert met as undergraduates at Georgetown University. Carla went on to receive a degree from the Fordham University School of Law; Robert studied medicine at Georgetown and practices ophthalmology. Their decision to have their wedding at the Plaza carried forward a family

FRED MARCUS

FRED MARCUS

tradition. In 1960, the bride's parents, Dr. and Mrs. Charles A. Straniero, were married in the Grand Ballroom. Two years later, Mrs. Straniero's brother, Paul Caputo, was married there as well.

On this occasion, the wedding guests entered a Grand Ballroom transformed into a sophisticated English garden by the adept hand of Atlas Floral Decorators. In this elegant setting, they dined on lobster and crab ravioli and chateaubriand, followed by quenelles of passion fruit and kiwi sorbet. An exquisite, tiered Plaza wedding cake provided the pièce de résistance.

The bride—resplendent in her mother's antique peau de soie, princess-style wedding gown and cathedral-length, hand-rolled silk veil—and the groom led off an evening of nonstop dancing with their first dance. Todd Stone and the Hank Lane Orchestra obliged with "It Had to Be You."

For their honeymoon, the newlyweds chose Venice and the islands of Santorini and Crete.

Allison Lambert / Howard Lutnick

When Allison Lambert and Howard Lutnick became engaged, they found themselves looking forward to planning their wedding. They took an intensely personal approach, working closely with everyone involved, to stage a wedding that would be essentially traditional but tailored in every aspect to reflect their own style and taste (which included holding a rehearsal dinner at the Metropolitan Museum of Art). Bride and groom knew exactly what they wanted, and each detail was customized with thought and care. The result was a traditional wedding that was unique.

Howard, who is president of the international investment firm Cantor Fitzgerald, and Allison, senior associate and litigator with the firm of Wilson, Elser, Moskowitz, Edelman & Dicker, selected the Bergdorf Goodman Bridal Registry as their main one, relying on Bloomingdale's and Tiffany & Co. for items not carried by Bergdorf. They were very impressed by Bergdorf's system of notification: When a guest chose a gift, a card would be sent describing the selection and offering the bridal couple the option of having the gift mailed wherever they wished; picking up the gift at the store; selecting a different item; or applying the credit to another area, such as silver or china, to complete a set.

For the wedding itself, Howard and Allison chose the Plaza.

On a Saturday evening in early December, guests arriving for the ceremony were directed to the Terrace Room. They entered through the Palm Court, closed to the public for the evening. On the top tier stood the *chuppah*, directly in front of the grotto. (The bottom tier was platformed to allow guests an unobstructed view.) Thousands of glowing candles, set in the trellised screen on the wall, offset white and champagne orchids, roses, and French tulips. On the floor, a special hand-painted gold runner led to the *chuppah*.

DENIS REGGIE

The bride wore a sleek, chantilly lace sheath embellished with crystals, pearls, caviar beads, and iridescent sequins. A multitiered tulle bustle complemented the back of the gown designed by Norma Lenain for Le Maison. The gown was chosen at Kleinfeld's. The bride's head-piece was a pearl-encrusted tiara with an attached five-yard-long train, sprinkled with clusters of pearls and sequins. The bouquet was composed of French roses and freesia in shades of champagne and white.

The two matrons of honor and ten bridesmaids wore floor-length black velvet dresses with evening gloves; the best man and ushers wore black tuxedos with white piqué vests and matching bow ties. A flower girl completed the wedding party.

The moving ceremony was performed by Cantor David Benedict, who has known the bride's family since the early 1970s, when he bar-mitzvahed both her brothers. Religious duties apart, the cantor is best known for his appearance years ago in the movie *Goodbye, Columbus.*

At the close of the ceremony, guests adjourned to the Palm Court. To ensure their privacy and create a feeling of warmth, it was enclosed by beautiful iridescent gold draperies. Within, hors d'oeuvres were served, butler-style. (The newlyweds had chosen not to have satel-lite buffets as they felt their guests might be less able to appreciate the meal to follow.)

The reception and dinner dance were held in the Grand Ballroom, where (as in the case of the Terrace Room and Palm Court), guests were greeted by the breathtaking decor of Anthony Ferraz of Anthony Ferraz Design. In the entrance to the Grand Ballroom, Ferraz installed champagne-colored draperies with gold centers between the columns. These were pulled back in graceful swags as guests entered. The tables were covered with iridescent copper tablecloths, topped by forty-five-inch-wide gold organza overlays festooned with fabric-covered buttons that matched the copper undercloths. The existing red carpet disappeared under a specially laid champagne-colored carpet, the red draperies were replaced with cham-pagne draperies, and the ceiling was tented in a sunburst design of white chiffon.

Centerpieces were five-foot-tall tripod stands supporting plateaus of pillars and candles. Champagne and white French tulips, roses, and orchids cascaded beneath the plateaus, carrying through the same theme that had been used in the Terrace Room. On each table stood three baroque tripods finished in antique gold, on which rested beeswax pillar candles. Ivory linen napkins, with gold-painted, hemstitched borders, were tied with gold organza ribbon. A cham-pagne rose was inserted into each. Gold ballroom chairs sporting white-and-gold-striped cush-ions completed the picture.

Two-hundred and fifty guests then dined on one of the Plaza's most select menus:

CAVIAR PRESENTATION OF BELUGA, OSETRA, AND SEVRUGA
(CHOICE OF STOLICHNAYA CRISTAL OR
CHASSAGNE-MONTRACHET, 1992)

RACK OF BABY LAMB PERSILLE
BLACK TRUFFLE SAUCE
POTATO NEST FILLED WITH PARISIENNE POTATOES
BUNDLE OF HARICOTS VERT TIED WITH LEEK RIBBON
(CHÂTEAU DUHART-MILAN, ROTHSCHILD, 1987)

WITH THE TOAST, LOUIS ROEDERER CRISTAL

BABY LETTUCE, RADICCHIO, ENDIVE
RASPBERRY VINAIGRETTE

DESSERT SAMPLER
CAPPUCCINO CUP WITH TIRAMISÙ

BEGGAR'S PURSE WITH APPLE PRALINE CRÈME CARAMEL
FRESH BERRIES SPRINKLED WITH GOLD DUST
CORDIALS
DEMITASSE
PETIT FOURS

ASSORTED CHOCOLATE-DIPPED FRUITS
INCLUDING STRAWBERRIES, APRICOTS, AND KIWIS
SUGAR-COATED GRAPES
MACAROONS
CHAMPAGNE TRUFFLES

The meal was fittingly concluded by Sylvia Weinstock's five-and-a-half-foot-tall wedding cake. A base of six layers of carrot cake supported columns (custom-designed to match columns in the couple's apartment), that in turn supported a top holding different sizes of burning beeswax pillar candles (that matched the centerpieces). Spilling down over the entire cake were masses of sugar tulips and roses in white, cream, and pale blush.

Because music would be a very important component of the event, Howard and Allison had invited Miles Herman of the Hank Lane Orchestra to their apartment well in advance of the wedding and reviewed the selections he intended to play throughout the evening. In this way they were assured that *all* the music would be to their liking, not merely their special requests. (Another critical issue: The decibel level was constantly monitored to allow for conversations at the tables.)

Bride and groom danced their first dance to Linda Ronstadt's "All My Life" on a specially installed dance floor hand-painted in champagne and white.

All in all, a spectacular and memorable wedding—and a clear tribute to the care with which it was planned and orchestrated.

DENIS REGGIE

Karen Jill Silverman / Dr. Leon Hodes

When the engagement of Karen Jill Silverman to Dr. Leon Hodes was announced, their respective families swung into action: The Silvermans met with top wedding consultant Barbara Feldman of the Barbara Feldman Organization and, in keeping with a tradition from his native Rhodesia, the groom's father began work on a poem to be read at the upcoming nuptials.

Above Right: KAREN AND HER FATHER, HOWARD SILVERMAN

The Silvermans felt strongly that a wedding is rooted in religion and therefore they desired their guests to be served kosher food. Ms. Feldman arranged for a tasting at the Plaza with Bert Leventhal of Newman & Leventhal Caterers. The offerings were exquisite:

BREAST OF POUSSIN IN PHYLLO TRUFFLE SAUCE
GOURMET CUCUMBER
(HOLLOWED TO RESEMBLE A NAPKIN RING)
FILLED WITH FIELD GREENS
GRILLED PLUM TOMATO WITH FINES HERBES
ONION CRACKLING FRITTER
BALSAMIC DIJON VINAIGRETTE DRESSING

NOISETTES OF BABY LAMB CHOP
WITH THE BONE SURMOUNTED BY CHOPS WITH
DARK RED WINE SAUCE
POTATO GALETTE WITH SHALLOTS AND TRUFFLES
FRESH ASPARAGUS, WHITE STRING BEANS,
AND BABY CARROTS WITH STEMS

POACHED PEAR
CHOCOLATE BOX WITH FRESH RASPBERRIES
MANGO SORBET WITH SPUN SUGAR LILY
SAUCES OF MANGO AND RASPBERRY IN A LACE EFFECT

PETIT FOURS
FRESH CHOCOLATE BASKET FILLED WITH MINTS

DEMITASSE

Each course was served with an accompanying wine.

On the day of the wedding, guests arrived at a Terrace Room transformed by Stephen Kolens of Atlas Floral Decorators. Three hundred large candles ringed the room. The aisle arrangements consisted of nine-foot-tall, thirteen-arm candelabra with Serina, Oclana, Message, Champagne, and Porcelina spray roses. (These were later transferred to the loge boxes

Nicole Mitchell / Eddie Murphy

Every wedding contains an element of drama, but when the bride is stunning model Nicole Mitchell and the groom is irrepressible comic Eddie Murphy—be prepared for something epic. Hundreds of fans and a horde of paparazzi strained behind police barricades to catch a glimpse of anything that could be seen. Inside, security was tight in the sealed-off Fifth Avenue lobby, where guests were carefully checked in and escorted to the Grand Ballroom.

Despite the momentous nature of the occasion, this was one husband-to-be who wasn't suffering from stage fright. (It's not every groom whose entrance reduces his guests to helpless laughter—then again, it's not every groom who appears wearing dark glasses and doing a Stevie Wonder impersonation.) Not to be outdone, three-year-old daughter Bria (the older of the couple's two children) took her turn at center stage, proudly leading a convoy of identically clad flower girls.

But on this night, it was Eddie's ravishing bride who stole the show. As Nicole emerged from the center box opposite the altar and started down the aisle on the arm of her father, five hundred guests suddenly broke into applause. The Grand Ballroom was transformed for the evening by floral designer Anthony Ferraz into a sea of pure white draperies, carpeting, and chairs. Creamy pastel roses, tulips, orchids, and tall, lit tapers covered balustrades along the aisle. The bride was resplendent in an Eve of Milady white silk and satin off-the-shoulder gown and twelve-foot cathedral train trimmed with rosettes, pearls, and Alençon lace. Her matching cathedral tulle veil was edged with Belgian embroidery and trimmed with iridescent Austrian crystals

Right: NICOLE, ON THE ARM OF HER FATHER, EDDIE MITCHELL

FRED MARCUS

FRED MARCUS

OPPOSITE: FRED MARCUS

and pearls. For her bouquet, Nicole carried a magnificent spray of white phalaenopsis orchids.

It was a traditional wedding with an unmistakably personal stamp. Nicole passed on *Lohengrin* and chose to walk down the aisle to her husband's composition "Don't Give Up on Love." Standing before an altar blanketed with branches from an enormous cherry blossom tree, the couple exchanged their vows in a classic double-ring ceremony. This didn't stop Eddie from whirling around to glower at his guests when the minister inquired if anyone knew a reason why the two should not be wed. (Which, needless to say, brought down the house.) At the conclusion of the ceremony, after the bride and groom's lingering embrace, Eddie gazed down at his daughter and lifted her into his arms. Bride, groom, and head flower girl made their way up the aisle to a standing ovation.

The ceremony over, family members, friends, and a host of celebrity guests joined the Murphys in the combined Terrace Room and Palm Court, where they were surrounded by pink rose trees and masses of pastel orchids, lilacs, gardenias, and tulips. A lavish menu included blini crepes with Russian caviar and medallions of lobster as an appetizer and an exquisite chicken dish with cognac sauce as an entree. Waiters bearing chilled bottles of Cristal kept champagne flutes filled.

Then it was back to the Grand Ballroom, where desserts were set out in the softly candlelit foyer. Nicole exchanged her fairy-tale gown for an alluring white, sequined dress and Eddie abandoned his tuxedo for a dark jacket and slacks. The room itself had undergone a second transformation. The white wonderland was now a disco, a tour de force of complex lighting concealed under billowing gauze draperies.

Once again tradition was observed: The bride's garter was deftly removed by the groom; she tossed her bouquet to a crowd of single women;

FRED MARCUS

Opposite: THE GRAND
BALLROOM TRANSFORMED
BY ANTHONY FERRAZ
INTO A DISCO.

Above: MEMBERS OF THE MITCHELL AND MURPHY FAMILIES.

FRED MARCUS

and the first slice was cut from Sylvia Weinstock's magnificent three-tier, 400-pound, five-foot-tall cake. Hundreds of pastel sugar flowers cascaded down over yellow cake filled with fresh strawberries, fresh banana filling and whipped cream; chocolate cake with mocha mousse filling; carrot cake with cream cheese filling; and yellow cake filled with lemon mousse and fresh raspberries. The top of the cake was adorned with two hummingbirds made of blown sugar.

Not surprisingly, music was a highlight at the Murphy nuptials and reflected the talents of the groom and a star-studded guest list. At Nicole's request, Karyn White sang a special version of her song "Tears of Joy" to the couple. The traditional first dance was to "Cuteness"—a song Eddie wrote just for Nicole.

The party was on. As dense fog drifted through the room and everything from soul to hip-hop resonated from the speakers, the Murphys and their guests danced till the small hours of the morning. As weddings go, it was a knockout production from start to finish.

FRED MARCUS

FRED MARCUS

FRED MARCUS

Top: SYLVIA WEINSTOCK'S THREE-TIER, FIVE-FOOT-TALL CAKE COMPRISED FOUR DIFFERENT CAKES AND FILLINGS, HUNDREDS OF SUGAR FLOWERS, AND WAS TOPPED WITH TWO BLOWN-SUGAR HUMMINGBIRDS.

Left: THE GROOM REMOVES THE GARTER

Wedding Announcements

If you live in a large city, chances are your newspaper receives more wedding announcements than it has room to print. You stand a better chance of yours being published if it is sent in at least three weeks in advance and includes all the details generally called for:

bride's full name
bride's parents' names
town where bride's parents live
bride's parents' occupations
bride's grandparents (both sets)
school and college bride attended
bride's occupation
groom's full name
town where groom lives
groom's parents' names
town where groom's parents live
groom's grandparents (both sets)
school and college groom attended
groom's occupation

date of wedding
ceremony and reception location
bride's attendants (note any relationship to bride or groom)
groom's attendants (note any relationship to bride or groom)
description of bridal gown
description of attendants' dresses
name of officiating clergy member
names of any soloists who performed at ceremony
honeymoon destination
town where couple plan to live after wedding

Newspapers use as much of the information as they wish to, and the editor may reword your announcement, but this is the basic format:

Miss Rachel Brynne Kamen was married yesterday to Mr. Peter Eric Dane. The marriage was performed at the Beekman Place Synagogue, New York City, by Rabbi Hillel Reiner.

The bride is the daughter of Mr. and Mrs. Marc Kamen of Manhattan. Her grandparents are Mr. and Mrs. Avi Kamen of Manhattan and the late Mr. and Mrs. Jeremy Reis of Johannesburg, South Africa.

Mr. Dane is the son of Mr. Gregory Dane of San Francisco, California, and the late Mrs. Dane. His grandparents are Mr. and Mrs. Zachary Dane of San Francisco, California, and Mrs. Renata Loeb and the late Mr. Loeb of Sausalito, California.

Mrs. Dane wore a white silk satin gown trimmed with fabric gardenias and carried a bouquet of gardenias.

Miss Talia Kamen served as her sister's maid of honor. The bridesmaids were Miss Natalie Dane, the groom's sister, Miss Ayisha Johnson, and Mrs. Mario Levi-Reiner. Francesca Levi-Reiner, daughter of Mr. and Mrs. Mario Levi-Reiner, was flower girl.

Mr. Dane's best man was Jonas Breitman of New York City. The ushers were Adam Kamen, the bride's brother; Marc Loeb, a cousin of the groom; and Harmon Cushing.

Mrs. Dane is a graduate of Stanford University and is an editor at Astor Press. Mr. Dane was graduated from Yale University and is a stage director.

The couple will live in New York City.

If you plan on keeping your maiden name after the wedding, you may indicate this in your announcement by saying, "The bride, who intends to keep her own name, is the daughter of . . ." Succeeding references would read "Ms. Kamen" or "the bride."

ERIC AND LISA BLUMENGRANZ

Financial Planning

KALMAN A. BARSON, CPA, CFE

Getting started together in married life is a very exciting experience. However, if not adequately prepared for financially, it can also be frightening and intimidating. The purpose of this chapter is to dispel some of the mysteries of beginning one's own financial life and to assist in making that a harmonious process for both newlyweds.

PAYING FOR YOUR OWN WEDDING

If you will be paying for your wedding, it will likely be the first large expense either one of you has encountered—outside of purchasing a car or paying college tuition. It is most helpful if you give yourself a comfortable time frame in which to save for the wedding. Plan the cost of the wedding well in advance, and then budget yourself to put away (preferably in a savings account specifically designated for this purpose) a certain amount every week or every month. If possible, both of you should contribute toward this account. Also, if both of you are going to contribute to the same one account, that account should require both of your signatures in order to withdraw money.

Be realistic as to what size wedding you can afford. While undoubtedly it is an event that you will forever remember, it isn't a good idea to start married life heavily in debt. Money pressures are often devastating to what was originally a successful and harmonious marriage. If you find it necessary to borrow, consider borrowing from family—which is often easier than borrowing through a bank, where credit checks and possibly collateral demands may present obstacles. On the other hand, be realistic as to your relationship with family, and understand the risk of straining that relationship by borrowing. Treat any such loan as an obligation that you must repay, just as if it were from a bank. Furthermore, expect to pay a fair rate of interest.

USING A BANK ACCOUNT

Opening up both a checking account and a savings account (or an interest-bearing checking or money market account) is essential for the proper handling of your money. It is important to keep funds liquid—readily available for whatever uses are necessary. Take pains to avoid bouncing checks. Don't write checks on money that isn't in the account, and be sure to reconcile your bank account each month. If you don't reconcile your account, you may find yourself issuing checks on funds that don't exist. If your control over funds is strong, you should also consider getting an overdraft privilege (or credit line) attached to your checking account. Simply put, with this protective mechanism in place, if you were to issue a check in excess of what was in your account (or against uncollected funds), the bank would nevertheless honor the check. The use of the overdraft privilege constitutes a loan—you are borrowing money from the bank. This should be paid back immediately, rather than allowing it to remain as a loan. This credit line, or overdraft privilege, should be treated as an exception to the rule—not as a handy way to get into debt. If used properly, it also will go a long way to establishing a favorable credit history.

ESTABLISHING YOUR CREDIT

One of the most valuable tools that you will be developing during the early years of your married life will be your credit rating. In many ways, it is very easy to establish a superior credit rating. Unfortunately, it is probably even easier to establish a bad credit rating. Paying your bills on time, which generally means buying within your limits and paying your debts, is about all you need to do to ensure a superior credit rating. The first time you fall behind in paying your credit card bill or the first time you miss a note payment on a loan from a bank or on a leased vehicle, you will have damaged your credit. A few such failings and you may cause serious damage to your credit rating; this will take years to rectify. Establish procedures so that you keep your bills organized and so that you make it a policy to pay them. Typically, most of us find it easy to pay our bills based on how we get paid—every week, every two weeks, every month—whatever works for you. Don't allow your desire for that hot new jacket or dinner at a fancy restaurant to prevent you from paying your utility bill on time.

Credit cards are a very important and convenient fact of life, but they must be respected for the harm they can cause you. Don't take out or accept every credit card offered to you, and don't take on more credit and more debt than you can comfortably handle. For most of us, one or two credit cards with sufficient credit lines will be more than adequate to meet any reasonable needs. Make it an absolute requirement that you pay your credit card in full every month—avoid wherever and whenever possible carrying a balance on your credit card. Not paying off your credit card every month is in effect borrowing money and paying for it at perhaps the highest interest rates legally charged in this country.

EMPLOYMENT AND COMPENSATION

Unless you are fortunate enough to be able to live off of a trust account, one or both people in a marriage will need to work—and probably for a long time. Too many times, when one gets a job, the W-4 form is filled out without thinking. No thought is given as to how many exemptions should be taken, and what the impact is on the net paycheck. If your gross pay is $500 a week, one of your most immediate questions is how much that will net—because it is only the net that is going to contribute directly toward covering your living expenses. Understand that the more exemptions you put on your W-4 form, the higher your paycheck will be. However, the greater your paycheck, the less taxes are withheld. Understand how those factors jointly work on what you will face on April 15 of each year—will you have enough taxes paid to cover your obligations, will you owe money, will you get a refund?

Recognize the unfortunate possibility of unemployment; another reason for savings is to provide for dry spells when there may be no regular income. Depending on your personal experiences and levels of skill and training, you may wish to spend (invest) money in training for either, or both, of you to broaden your skills. This will further protect you from possible unemployment and enhance your reemployment opportunities.

BUDGETING

One of the most overlooked planning tools of a young marriage is establishing a budget—and keeping to it. The two of you should sit down and spend some time talking about what your various living needs are—rent, utilities, telephone, cable TV, clothing, vacations, schooling, note payments, and so on. Go through the past year or so of your checking accounts or bills to get ideas as to all the items that constitute your financial life and how much they truly cost. Keep in mind that your costs include income and Social Security taxes. One of your required "expenditures" should be contributions to a savings or investment account. At the end of this chapter, you will find a suggested format for developing a budget. Fill this out, or use it as a template to create your own budget.

There are many different systems for budgeting your money—any or all of them can work if you are willing to let them. One simple, but reliable, approach is the envelope system. From every paycheck, you put away some money in an envelope for rent, in another envelope for food, in another envelope for the car loan, and so forth. At the end of every month, in theory, you have put away enough money to make that payment or cover those expenses. Make sure there is an envelope for savings.

SAVINGS AND RETIREMENT PLANS

It is vital to save. Start a savings plan and contribute to it on a regular basis. Try not to use it for any type of normal living expenses—give it a chance to build up and serve as a base for such major purchases as a house or a business, or to cover an emergency situation. As soon as you are in a financial position to do so, start putting money into some form of retirement plan. If your employer offers a 401(k) plan, contribute to it—as much as you can. If not, by all means put $2,000 a year into an IRA (generally a tax-deductible contribution). You get a tax deduction for saving money instead of spending it.

Unless you have adequate funds and are financially sophisticated, do not go lightly into the stock market or into the hands of a financial adviser/counselor/planner who would have you putting money in any investment other than a safe liquid one. It is not that you should never invest in the stock market—in the long run that has often proved to be an excellent place to invest. However, it is not something for novices or for those who do not have excess funds. Take it upon yourself to learn about the stock market and mutual funds by reading any of the substantial literature that is available, and subscribe to one or two financial-oriented consumer magazines. If you do invest in the stock market, *absolutely* never give transactional discretion to any broker. All transactions must require your approval. This will protect you from the relatively few dishonest or overly self-serving brokers.

INSURANCE

Insurance is one of those expenditures that hopefully will be "wasted." The problem is, you don't know in advance if it will be wasted, and if it turns out to be needed, not having it can be extremely expensive. There are a few types of insurance that you will need to deal with—health, property and casualty, auto, disability, and life insurance.

Health insurance is, for many, virtually taken for granted, since businesses often provide full or partial coverage to their employees. If you or your spouse are not employed by a company that provides medical insurance, you need to consider your options—purchasing medical insurance privately, or possibly through a group or association with which you or a close relative may be connected. This can be expensive and, as with many other insurances, the greater the deductible (the higher the threshold necessary before the insurance begins coverage) the cheaper the insurance. It is not unusual for young couples to feel they do not need medical insurance—you are probably at the healthiest time of your lives. However, it only takes one accident or one surprise illness to cause you not only significant and substantial medical expenses, but possibly compound that by also putting you out of work for a period of time.

Casualty and property insurance for most people typically means homeowners or renters insurance. Its purpose is to protect your property from damage, theft, and the like, and it generally includes personal liability insurance. Auto insurance is probably required in every state of the country—though the rules vary considerably. Concerns include coverage for property damage to your automobile, medical coverage for yourself or other people involved in any accident, and liability relating to automobile accidents. This can be expensive—especially if you are young, and especially if you live in a high accident area or in certain densely populated cities. However, in most areas it is illegal to drive without at least liability insurance, and in many cases it is foolish to drive without casualty insurance—unless your car is worth little more than its scrap value.

Umbrella, or excess, liability insurance often is not needed for a young couple. This type of policy gives you extra liability coverage in the event that there is a major catastrophe for which you are found liable—for instance, if somebody were to fall in your apartment and suffer a debilitating injury. Of course, not having this type of insurance can put you into bankruptcy if such an unusual accident were to happen.

Too often overlooked by young couples, but in reality far more important than life insurance, is disability insurance. The chances of someone in his or her twenties becoming disabled over the next thirty years, are far greater than of that person dying. And, if disabled, your need for money increases, while at the same time your ability to generate that money might decrease or be eliminated.

Keep in mind that life insurance is *absolutely not* a savings vehicle or a form of investment. Its purpose is to provide your dependents—those who rely upon your income—with a cushion in the event of your death. For a young couple with no children, and perhaps only an apartment and no mortgage, life insurance is probably unnecessary. If you are considering purchasing life insurance, consider only the cheapest insurance available—term insurance.

BUYING THAT BIG TICKET ITEM

There will be a time in your married life when you will need to deal with buying a large item— a car, or a home, or an apartment. Essentially, there are two ways of buying these—either you have the money to buy them outright, or you borrow. In order to have the money, most of us need to have a planned system of savings so that we may gradually build the pool of funds necessary to make such a purchase. That should be a specific, targeted goal. Indeed, the two of you need to have discussed in advance what your goals are for many aspects of your married life—not the least of which is the handling of such a major purchase.

You can expect that some part of the cost of a car, and a significant part of the cost of a house, will require borrowing. In most situations, the money will be borrowed from a bank or mortgage company or some other lending institution—as contrasted with coming from family. You will have made obtaining a loan/mortgage much easier if you have maintained a good credit rating. When the time comes to look for a mortgage, be sure to shop around. There are many different deals available, rates will vary depending on who is lending the money, and the costs of borrowing (points up front, closing costs, and the like) will vary significantly. Be realistic as to what you can afford.

CHILDREN

Make no mistake about it, children are a delight—and an expense. Recognize when you get married that having children often is a double hit on your income. First, typically you lose at least part, if not all, of the income power of one of you, at least for a while. Second, that child represents a very real and significant expense. You should plan, financially, for the birth of a child by building up the appropriate financial reserves. A child

should be a benefit to a marriage, not a burden or an ever-present source of financial strain. In addition, while it is not unusual for both spouses to continue working after the birth of a child, you must not overlook the cost of dependent care—if neither spouse is going to stay home with the child on a full-time basis, you will need to hire someone or some group to take care of that child, unless you are fortunate enough to have family that would be willing to do it.

TAX RETURNS

Now that you are married, filing tax returns will likely change slightly. When you were single, each of you filed your own tax return—as a single individual. Once married, you effectively have two ways of filing—either married filing jointly, or married filing separately. Most of the time, married filing separately is inadvisable because it will generally cost you more in taxes to file separately than it would to file jointly. However, it very well may cost you more filing jointly than it did filing as single individuals. This is often referred to as the marriage penalty in our tax system. This penalty can be significant if your incomes are approximately comparable and relatively significant. Filing a joint return is not always advisable. It is voluntary, not mandatory. Note that from a tax point of view, whether or not you are considered married is solely a function of your marital status as of the last day of the year. If you marry on December 31, you are considered married for that year.

Filing jointly is the most common way for married people to file tax returns, something that is done virtually automatically. However, there are pitfalls. When you file jointly, you are assuming full and total personal liability for all taxes that may come about from that tax return. The IRS is not in any way obligated to seek a tax only from the person who accrued it, or who lied or misrepresented on a tax return. With only certain exceptions (which are too esoteric for the purposes of this book), each party to a joint return is equally and totally liable for all liabilities arising from that tax return. This may be of significant concern—especially if one of you is in a cash business and not reporting all of his/her income. Or if one of you takes unusually aggressive positions as to deductions.

There are three ways to take care of your annual tax filing: You can do it yourself; you can use a storefront operation; or you can use a full-time tax professional such as a CPA or an accountant. Most people are capable of doing their own—particularly when the return is relatively simple. However, unless you are willing to pay attention to the rules and actually spend time understanding the tax return booklet from the IRS and your local state, you should consider using a paid service. If your return is truly simple, and little more than a W-2 and an interest statement, a storefront operation will probably do a creditable job. On the other hand, if you have some complexity—your own business, stock market transactions, rental properties, or other complicating issues—it is strongly recommended that you go to a full-time professional.

SEPARATE ASSETS

Starting off together, it is natural to believe that everything will be owned jointly and that regardless of where the money comes from, you will be sharing everything. In all likelihood that will be the case. However, there is at least one type of asset that, even in the most jointly cooperative situation, should either be kept separate or at least be recognized as something worthy of special consideration. I'm referring to gifts and inheritances from family. This is not the $50 or $100 annual birthday gift, but rather a $10,000 estate planning type gift, and particularly inheritances. In most states, you will find that these types of assets, as long as they are maintained separately, are entitled to special treatment as one's own separate asset. If in your particular situation this represents something of significant value, you may wish to engage legal and financial counsel.

CHRISTINA AND MICHAEL FORSTER

PRENUPTIAL AGREEMENT

If one or both of you come from a family with significant wealth, or if this is a marriage later on in life and one or both of you have already built up some wealth, you should at least consider the merit of a prenuptial (also referred to as antenuptial) agreement. The purpose of such an agreement is to protect the assets of the person with a fair amount of personal or family wealth.

The validity and enforceability of such an agreement varies widely from state to state. However, the basic rules to making a prenuptial agreement enforceable are that there be full disclosure as to each of your respective financial situations, that there be separate legal representation for each of you, and that there is no pressure or coercion in signing the agreement. Any such agreement requires competent legal counsel

Budget

	PER WEEK	PER MONTH
Mortgage/rent	$	$
Parking fee		
Real estate taxes		
Home insurance		
Electric and gas		
Oil		
Wood		
Repairs and maintenance		
Water and sewer		
Garbage removal		
Snow removal		
Lawn care		
Maintenance charges (condo/co-op)		
Exterminator		
Telephone		
Service contracts on equipment		
Cable TV		
Appliance replacement		
Furniture replacement		
Other loans		
Federal income taxes		
Social Security taxes		
State and local income taxes		
Personal auto—payments/replacements		
Insurance		

Budget

	PER WEEK	PER MONTH
Maintenance	$	$
Gasoline		
Commuting expense		
Food at home		
Household supplies		
Prescription drugs		
Nonprescription drugs and vitamins		
Toiletries and cosmetics		
Restaurants		
Clothing		
Dry cleaning/laundry		
Hair care		
Domestic help/maid		
Medical—unreimbursed		
Dental and orthodontic—unreimbursed		
Eyeglasses and contacts		
Medical insurance		
Disability insurance		
Life insurance		
Club dues and membership		
Sports, hobbies, and collecting		
Tapes and records		
Savings		
Vacations		
Adult education		

PERSONAL
WEDDING PLANNER

Major Holidays

Note: Be sure to check your selected date against a current religious calendar.

HOLIDAYS IN 1996

Monday, January 1—New Year's Day

Monday, January 15—Martin Luther King, Jr., Day

Monday, February 19—Washington-Lincoln Day

Wednesday, February 21—Ash Wednesday

Tuesday, March 5—Purim

Sunday, March 17—St. Patrick's Day

Thursday, April 4, through Thursday, April 11—Passover

Friday, April 5—Good Friday

Sunday, April 7—Easter

Sunday, May 12—Mother's Day

Friday, May 24, and Saturday, May 25—Shavuoth

Monday, May 27—Memorial Day observed

Sunday, June 16—Father's Day

Thursday, July 4—Independence Day

Monday, September 2—Labor Day

Saturday, September 14—Rosh Hashanah

Monday, September 23—Yom Kippur

Saturday, September 28, and Sunday, September 29—Succoth

Monday, October 14—Columbus Day observed

Tuesday, November 5—Election Day

Monday, November 11—Veterans Day

Thursday, November 28—Thanksgiving Day

Friday, December 6, through Friday, December 13—Hanukkah

Wednesday, December 25—Christmas

HOLIDAYS IN 1997

Wednesday, January 1—New Year's Day

Monday, January 20—Martin Luther King, Jr., Day

Wednesday, February 12—Ash Wednesday

Monday, February 17—Washington-Lincoln Day

Monday, March 17—St. Patrick's Day

Sunday, March 23, and Monday, March 24—Purim

Friday, March 28—Good Friday

Sunday, March 30—Easter

Tuesday, April 22, through Tuesday, April 29—Passover

Sunday, May 11—Mother's Day

Monday, May 26—Memorial Day observed

Wednesday, June 11, and Thursday, June 12—Shavuoth

Sunday, June 15—Father's Day

Friday, July 4—Independence Day

Monday, September 1—Labor Day

Thursday, October 2—Rosh Hashanah

Saturday, October 11—Yom Kippur

Monday, October 13—Columbus Day
observed

Thursday, October 16, and Friday,
October 17—Succoth

Tuesday, November 4—Election Day

Tuesday, November 11—Veterans Day

Thursday, November 27—Thanksgiving
Day

Wednesday, December 24, through
Wednesday, December 31—Hanukkah

Thursday, December 25—Christmas

HOLIDAYS IN 1998

Thursday, January 1—New Year's Day

Monday, January 19—Martin Luther King,
Jr., Day

Monday, February 16—Washington-Lincoln
Day

Wednesday, February 25—Ash Wednesday

Friday, March 13, and Saturday, March 14—
Purim

Tuesday, March 17—St. Patrick's Day

Friday, April 10—Good Friday

Saturday, April 11, through Saturday, April
18—Passover

Sunday, April 12—Easter

Sunday, May 10—Mother's Day

Monday, May 25—Memorial Day observed

Sunday, May 31, and Monday, June 1—
Shavuoth

Sunday, June 21—Father's Day

Saturday, July 4—Independence Day

Monday, September 7—Labor Day

Monday, September 21—Rosh Hashanah

Wednesday, September 30—Yom Kippur

Monday, October 5, and Tuesday, October
6—Succoth

Monday, October 12—Columbus Day

Tuesday, November 3—Election Day

Wednesday, November 11—Veterans Day

Thursday, November 26—Thanksgiving
Day

Monday, December 14, through Monday,
December 21—Hanukkah

Friday, December 25—Christmas

HOLIDAYS IN 1999

Friday, January 1—New Year's Day

Monday, January 18—Martin Luther King, Jr., Day

Monday, February 15—Washington-Lincoln Day

Wednesday, February 17—Ash Wednesday

Tuesday, March 2, and Wednesday, March 3—Purim

Wednesday, March 17—St. Patrick's Day

Thursday, April 1, through Thursday, April 8—Passover

Friday, April 2—Good Friday

Sunday, April 4—Easter

Sunday, May 9—Mother's Day

Friday, May 21, and Saturday, May 22—Shavuoth

Monday, May 31—Memorial Day observed

Sunday, June 20—Father's Day

Sunday, July 4—Independence Day

Monday, September 6—Labor Day

Saturday, September 11—Rosh Hashanah

Monday, September 20—Yom Kippur

Saturday, September 25, and Sunday, September 26—Succoth

Monday, October 11—Columbus Day observed

Tuesday, November 2—Election Day

Thursday, November 11—Veterans Day

Thursday, November 25—Thanksgiving Day

Saturday, December 4, through Saturday, December 11—Hanukkah

Saturday, December 25—Christmas

HOLIDAYS IN 2000

Saturday, January 1—New Year's Day

Monday, January 17—Martin Luther King, Jr., Day

Monday, February 21—Washington-Lincoln Day

Wednesday, March 8—Ash Wednesday

Friday, March 17—St. Patrick's Day

Tuesday, March 21, and Wednesday, March 22—Purim

Thursday, April 20, through Thursday, April 27—Passover

Friday, April 21—Good Friday

Sunday, April 23—Easter

Sunday, May 14—Mother's Day

Monday, May 29—Memorial Day observed

Friday, June 9, and Saturday, June 10—Shavuoth

Sunday, June 18—Father's Day

Tuesday, July 4—Independence Day

Monday, September 4—Labor Day

Saturday, September 30—Rosh Hashanah

Monday, October 9—Columbus Day observed

Monday, October 9—Yom Kippur

Saturday, October 14, and Sunday, October 15—Succoth

Tuesday, November 7—Election Day

Saturday, November 11—Veterans Day

Thursday, November 23—Thanksgiving Day

Friday, December 22, through Friday, December 29—Hanukkah

Monday, December 25—Christmas

HOLIDAYS IN 2001

Monday, January 1—New Year's Day

Monday, January 15—Martin Luther King, Jr., Day

Monday, February 19—Washington-Lincoln Day

Wednesday, February 28—Ash Wednesday

Friday, March 9, and Saturday, March 10—Purim

Saturday, March 17—St. Patrick's Day

Sunday, April 8, through Sunday, April 15—Passover

Friday, April 13—Good Friday

Sunday, April 15—Easter

Sunday, May 13—Mother's Day

Monday, May 28, and Tuesday, May 29—Shavuoth

Monday, May 28—Memorial Day observed

Sunday, June 17—Father's Day

Wednesday, July 4—Independence Day

Monday, September 3—Labor Day

Tuesday, September 18—Rosh Hashanah

Thursday, September 27—Yom Kippur

Tuesday, October 2, and Wednesday, October 3—Succoth

Monday, October 8—Columbus Day observed

Tuesday, November 6—Election Day

Sunday, November 11—Veterans Day

Thursday, November 22—Thanksgiving Day

Monday, December 10, through Monday, December 17—Hanukkah

Tuesday, December 25—Christmas

Bride's Timetable

———

*O*NE YEAR TO SIX MONTHS IN ADVANCE:

- Decide style of wedding ceremony and reception
- Select date and time of day
- Hire bridal consultant (optional)
- Decide location for ceremony and reception; reserve both

- Confirm availability of person officiating
- Decide on number of guests
- Decide on bridal party and ask them to serve
- Order invitations, enclosures, announcements, and stationery

Calendar

———

NINE MONTHS BEFORE WEDDING

....

....

....

....

....

....

....

....

....

....

....

*S*IX MONTHS TO THREE MONTHS IN ADVANCE:

∝ If you are having a religious ceremony, meet with clergy member to discuss details and procedures

∝ Select and order bridal gown; arrange for fittings

∝ Select and order attendants' gowns; arrange for fittings

∝ Prepare guest lists

∝ Hire floral designer

∝ Book musicians and/or disk jockey

∝ Select photographer and videographer

∝ Select baker for wedding cake

SIX MONTHS BEFORE WEDDING

FIVE MONTHS BEFORE WEDDING

FOUR MONTHS BEFORE WEDDING

THREE MONTHS BEFORE WEDDING

*T*WO MONTHS IN ADVANCE:

- ✑ Arrange for the bridal party's transportation to the ceremony and reception
- ✑ Decide on dinner service, silver, and stemware patterns and list selections for bridal registry
- ✑ Check on fittings and accessories for attendants
- ✑ Finalize selection of linens, draperies, lighting scheme, floral arrangements, bouquets, etc., with floral designer
- ✑ Select music for ceremony and reception
- ✑ Work out details and arrangements with photographer and videographer
- ✑ Finalize menu and other arrangements for reception

- ✑ Decide on wedding cake flavor and style
- ✑ See hairdresser to try out style for wedding
- ✑ See makeup artist for consultation
- ✑ Select wedding rings
- ✑ Collect information on accommodations for out-of-town guests (reserve block of rooms if necessary)
- ✑ Arrange for housing of out-of-town attendants
- ✑ Address and stuff invitations
- ✑ Mail invitations six weeks before wedding date
- ✑ Check to make certain groom and groomsmen have arranged for formal wear

TWO MONTHS BEFORE WEDDING

WEEK OF

MONDAY

....

....

....

....

TUESDAY

....

....

....

....

WEDNESDAY

....

....

....

....

THURSDAY

....

....

....

....

FRIDAY

....

....

....

....

SATURDAY

....

....

....

....

SUNDAY

....

....

....

....

SEVEN WEEKS BEFORE WEDDING

WEEK OF ....

MONDAY

TUESDAY

WEDNESDAY

THURSDAY

FRIDAY

SATURDAY

....

....

....

....

SUNDAY

....

....

....

....

SIX WEEKS BEFORE WEDDING

WEEK OF

MONDAY

TUESDAY

WEDNESDAY

THURSDAY

FRIDAY

SATURDAY

....
....
....
....
....

SUNDAY

....
....
....
....
....

FIVE WEEKS BEFORE WEDDING

WEEK OF ....

MONDAY

....
....
....
....

TUESDAY

....
....
....

WEDNESDAY

....
....
....

THURSDAY

....
....
....

FRIDAY

....
....
....
....

SATURDAY
....
....
....
....

SUNDAY
....
....
....
....
....

*O*NE MONTH IN ADVANCE:

- Arrange for blood tests and marriage license
- Record gifts; write thank you notes
- Decide on honeymoon clothing
- Double-check on bridal and attendants' accessories
- Make final arrangements with floral designer, musicians, wedding cake baker, banquet manager, photographer, videographer, etc.
- If taking groom's last name, arrange for name change on pertinent documents
- Arrange for bridesmaids' luncheon
- Address and stamp announcements for mailing the day after wedding
- Make out seating plan for bridal party and parents' tables
- Work out tentative seating plan for guests
- Send wedding announcement to newspapers
- Arrange for wedding rehearsal, rehearsal dinner; notify bridal party
- Make hair, makeup, manicure, pedicure appointments

FOUR WEEKS BEFORE WEDDING

WEEK OF

MONDAY

TUESDAY

WEDNESDAY

THURSDAY

....
....
....
....

FRIDAY

....
....
....
....

SATURDAY

....
....
....

SUNDAY

....
....
....
....

THREE WEEKS BEFORE WEDDING

WEEK OF

MONDAY

TUESDAY

WEDNESDAY

THURSDAY

FRIDAY

SATURDAY ....

....

....

....

SUNDAY ....

....

....

....

....

*T*WO WEEKS IN ADVANCE:

∞ Confirm all lodging arrangements | ∞ Confirm details with floral designer, banquet manager, and others

TWO WEEKS BEFORE WEDDING

WEEK OF

MONDAY

....

....

....

....

TUESDAY

....

....

....

....

WEDNESDAY

....

....

....

....

THURSDAY

....

....

....

....

FRIDAY

....
....
....
....

SATURDAY

....
....
....
....

SUNDAY

....
....
....
....

*O*NE WEEK IN ADVANCE:

∞ **Buy gifts for attendants**
∞ **Buy gift for groom**

∞ **Give final guest count to banquet manager**

ONE WEEK BEFORE WEDDING

DAY

4 DAYS BEFORE WEDDING

DAY

3 DAYS BEFORE WEDDING

DAY

*O*NE OR TWO DAYS IN ADVANCE:

∞ **Have manicure, pedicure**

ONE TO TWO DAYS BEFORE WEDDING

*W*EDDING DAY—MORNING:

∞ Have hair done
∞ Check on any orders not being delivered to see that they've been picked up

*T*WO HOURS BEFORE CEREMONY:

∞ Dresser and/or attendants to arrive wherever you are dressing

*O*NE HOUR BEFORE CEREMONY:
∞ Have makeup done
∞ Dress
∞ Ushers should arrive at place of ceremony

*O*NE HALF HOUR BEFORE CEREMONY:

∞ Groom and best man should arrive at place of ceremony
∞ Background music begins
∞ Guests begin arriving and are seated
∞ Best man checks last-minute arrangements and gives officiating clergy or justice honorarium
∞ Family members and honored guests are seated "within the ribbon" or in pews near front

*F*IVE MINUTES BEFORE CEREMONY:

∞ Groom's parents arrive, mother is escorted to her seat, followed by her husband
∞ Bride's mother is escorted to her seat in the front row
∞ White carpet, or aisle runner, rolled down the aisle
∞ Bride's father takes his place with bride
∞ Attendants take their places in proper order for processional
∞ Music starts and ushers lead procession down the aisle

WEDDING DAY

....

....

....

....

....

....

MASTER CHECKLIST

OFFICIATING CLERGY OR JUSTICE OF THE PEACE
....
....
....

CATERER
....
....
....

MENU
....
....
....

WEDDING CAKE
....
....
....

LIQUOR
....
....
....

FLOWERS
....
....
....

MUSIC
....
....
....

INVITATIONS AND STATIONERY
....
....
....

BRIDAL ATTIRE: BRIDE, GROOM, ATTENDANTS
....
....
....

WEDDING RINGS

....

....

....

PHOTOGRAPHY

....

....

....

VIDEOGRAPHY

....

....

....

NEWSPAPER ANNOUNCEMENTS

....

....

....

BRIDAL REGISTRY

....

....

....

MARRIAGE LICENSE AND BLOOD TESTS

....

....

....

NAME CHANGE DETAILS (IF REQUIRED)

....

....

....

PREWEDDING DINNERS OR PARTIES

....

....

....

REHEARSAL/REHEARSAL DINNER

....

....

....

....

SEATING PLANS

....

....

....

ATTENDANTS' GIFTS

....

....

OUT-OF-TOWN ATTENDANTS AND GUESTS

....

....

TRANSPORTATION

....

....

TROUSSEAU

....

....

HONEYMOON PLANS

....

....

RECEIVING LINE

....

....

BRIDAL PARTY

Maid of honor ....

Matron of honor ....

Bridesmaid ....

Bridesmaid ....

Bridesmaid ....

Bridesmaid ....

Bridesmaid ....

Junior bridesmaid ....

Flower girl ....

Best man ....

Usher ....

Usher ....

Usher ....

Usher ....

Usher ....

Junior usher ....

Ring bearer ....

Page ....

GIFTS FOR ATTENDANTS

INVITATIONS

WORDING:

....

....

....

....

....

ENCLOSURES:

....

....

....

....

ENVELOPES/RETURN ADDRESS:

....

....

....

....

PAPER STOCK: ....

INK: ....

TYPEFACE: ....

ENCLOSURES: ....

NUMBER ORDERED: ....

ORDERED FROM: ....   TELEPHONE: ....   DATE: ....

DELIVERY DATE: ....

WEDDING ANNOUNCEMENTS

WORDING:

....

....

....

....

....

....

....

....

....

NEWSPAPER ....

....

EDITOR ....

....

ADDRESS ....

....

FAX NO. ....

....

TEL. NO. ....

....

SENT ....

....

BRIDAL GOWN

DESCRIPTION: ....

COLOR: ....

SIZE: ....

MANUFACTURER/STYLE NUMBER: ....

STORE: ....

SALESPERSON: ....

TELEPHONE: ....

COST: ....

DEPOSIT: ....

BALANCE: ....

DATE ORDERED: ....

DATE REQUIRED: ....

FIRST FITTING: ....

TIME: ....

ADDRESS: ....

TELEPHONE: ....

PERSON MAKING ALTERATIONS: ....

SECOND FITTING: ....

TIME: ....

FINAL FITTING: ....

TIME: ....

HEADPIECE

DESCRIPTION: ....

COLOR: ....

MANUFACTURER/STYLE NUMBER: ....

STORE: ....

SALESPERSON: ....

TELEPHONE: ....

COST: ....

DEPOSIT: ....

BALANCE: ....

DATE ORDERED: ....

DATE REQUIRED: ....

VEIL

DESCRIPTION: ....

COLOR: ....

MANUFACTURER/STYLE NUMBER: ....

STORE: ....

SALESPERSON: ....

TELEPHONE: ....

COST: ....

DEPOSIT: ....

BALANCE: ....

DATE ORDERED: ....

DATE REQUIRED: ....

ACCESSORIES

UNDERCLOTHES ....

SLIP ....

HOSIERY ....

SHOES ....

BACKUP PAIR (PUMPS HALF-SIZE LARGER/BALLET SLIPPERS) ....

....

GARTER ....

GLOVES ....

JEWELRY ....

HAIR ORNAMENTS ....

OTHER ....

SAMPLE MASTER GUEST, MAILING, AND GIFT LIST

NAME ....

ADDRESS ....

TELEPHONE   (HOME) ....

            (WORK) ....

            (WEEKEND) ....

FAX ....

NAME ....

ADDRESS ....

TELEPHONE   (HOME) ....

            (WORK) ....

            (WEEKEND) ....

FAX ....

NAME ....

ADDRESS ....

TELEPHONE   (HOME) ....

            (WORK) ....

            (WEEKEND) ....

FAX ....

SAMPLE GIFT LIST

FROM: ....

GIFT: ....

RECEIVED: .... THANK YOU: ....

FROM: ....

GIFT: ....

RECEIVED: .... THANK YOU: ....

FROM: ....

GIFT: ....

RECEIVED: .... THANK YOU: ....

FROM: ....

GIFT: ....

RECEIVED: .... THANK YOU: ....

FROM: ....

GIFT: ....

RECEIVED: .... THANK YOU: ....

FROM: ....

GIFT: ....

RECEIVED: .... THANK YOU: ....